Go, Be Loving

You Don't Have To Wait To Be Loved

Go, Be Loving

You Don't Have To Wait To Be Loved

Jonquil Hinds

BOOKS

Winchester, UK
Washington, USA

First published by O-Books, 2012
O-Books is an imprint of John Hunt Publishing Ltd., Laurel House, Station Approach,
Alresford, Hants, SO24 9JH, UK
office1@o-books.net
www.o-books.com

For distributor details and how to order please visit the 'Ordering' section on our website.

Text copyright: Jonquil Hinds 2010

ISBN: 978 1 84694 382 9

A CIP catalogue record for this book is available from the British Library.

Design: Thomas Davies

Printed in the UK by CPI Antony Rowe
Printed in the USA by Offset Paperback Mfrs, Inc

We operate a distinctive and ethical publishing philosophy in all
areas of our business, from our global network of authors to
production and worldwide distribution.

CONTENTS

Acknowledgements

I would like to thank everyone – my family, my friends, my counsellees, my various guides and counsellors – with whom I have come in touch in the course of my life. They have all contributed to my growing and thus to the developing of my ideas about loving. However, without the constant support and encouragement of Melanie Bray and Tom Hinds and the occasional prods by Sarah Coles my idea would never have become a book. My heartfelt thanks to them.

I would also like to thank those of my friends who have given of their IT skills – mine being limited.

I have written the facts of my own life are as I have perceived them. The names and narratives of counsellees have been mixed up so that neither they nor anyone else could recognize them for sure, though many people have had the same, or similar, experiences.

Preface

Brian Thorne,
Emeritus Professor of Counselling,
University of East Anglia, 2007

This book starts from the undeniable fact that there are countless people in the world who believe that they are both unloved and unlovable. From such a belief comes intense loneliness and often much shame. It is also a belief which can endure for a life time.

Jonquil Hinds writes from the perspective of someone who has herself entertained this belief but who at the age of 50 made the courageous decision to face it and to set about releasing herself from its power. Her discoveries have not only trans-formed her life but have provided the material for a book which constitutes a remarkable treatise on love in action. With metic-ulous attention to the detailed exploration of the ways in which human-beings deny and are denied the liberating power of love in their lives, she provides her readers with a remarkable message of hope. Her concept of GO-BI loving (Going Out in self-giving and Bringing In) has its origin in the simple realization that the activity of loving is not dependent on the experience of being loved. The lover is in control of his or her loving and does not even need the beloved to be aware of being loved for a complete flow of loving to be achieved.

From this simple - but revolutionary - insight Jonquil Hinds develops a profound theory and practice of loving which will speak to all those who struggle to be free of the fears and obstacles to intimacy which ruin so many lives. Her vignettes and anecdotes also provide much material for those counsellors and others whose task it is to come alongside those who suffer the intense loneliness which characterizes the experience of anyone who has found little love and despairs of ever offering it to others. This essentially practical book is at the same time a book which makes the spirit sing.

Introduction

What Is Loving?

Millions of words have been spoken, sung and written about love. The Greeks had seven words for it but they all describe different sorts of people or things that we can love. They don't actually describe what loving is. At the age of fifty I found myself asking this most fundamental of questions and not finding an answer, or at any rate not one that satisfied me. I have an enquiring mind, so once I had dared to ask the question: 'What is loving?' others came hot on its heels: 'How do we do it?', 'What are the obstacles to doing it?', 'How do we overcome them?'.

This book is about the answers I found to those questions, and a host of others that arose as I grappled with the first four.

Even the questions did not arrive, fully formed, in my head. I simply knew that I did not know anything about this thing called love; what it was or how to do it. All I knew was that I felt, and always had felt, unloved. And I had a vague idea that loving and being loved was what life was all about, so if at this late stage I wanted to get a life, I had better start by finding out about the thing that people called love.

Some form of loving, leading to a state of losing ourselves in the beloved, seemed to be the goal of most of the world's great mystical writers, so it must be of ultimate significance. The problem, for me, was that most of these writers seemed to join the traveller once he or she was already on the road. I desperately needed to know how to get started.

I found an answer in a simple little doodle, the top one on the cover of this book, which has evolved over the last fifteen years, of a little Green person Going Out in self-giving and Bringing In, or receiving a little Blue person. The acronym gave me GO-BI and the movement became known as GO-BI loving.

Part 1

Chapter I

The Birth of an Idea

I Had a Problem

I believed I was unloved. I also believed I was unlovable; and I didn't know what to do about it. Lots of people feel unloved and unlovable; it's not that unusual. However, when I became aware that I felt that way, I did not know it was a common state to be in. I felt intensely alone and deeply ashamed of being alone. Lonely people seem to fall into one of two groups: either they believe their loneliness is all their own fault, or they believe it is everyone else's. I belong to the former group but, which ever group we belong to, we all feel equal despair. Some of us feel we can't change ourselves, while others discover that they surely can't change other people, however hard they try.

Love didn't seem to be a part of my life, so that made me feel that there must be something seriously wrong with me as a person. I felt that life was simply not worth living – unless I did something about it. I didn't know what to do, and a part of me was afraid to do anything anyway.

I have noticed, in the course of my life, that I always need some significant event to kick start me into taking a new direction. The event that got me going this time was the death of Tin, a dearly loved cat, who had lived with me for eight years. I was devastated by her loss. Thinking, during the night before I buried her, how much she had meant to me I realized the loveless-ness of the rest of my life. Believing myself unloved and unlovable by people, I had put all of myself into a relationship with a cat. 'How sad is that?' I asked myself.

4

I took a deep breath ... and decided to do something about it. The 'something' was to sign up for a counselling course, which I had been thinking about for ages anyway. This meant that I also had to go into personal counselling. It was pretty scary because I had never before talked about my deep feelings, or any feelings for that matter. During the process of unpacking myself I discovered that I felt that my mother had not loved me, and that, deep inside myself, I had decided that if Mummy didn't love me, then neither would, nor could, anybody else. That seemed to be the problem in a nutshell. But what to do about it?

On the counselling course I found myself studying psychology which told me that we learn to love by being loved. This, of course, is broadly true but its inevitable implication for me seemed to be that if I had not been loved, I would never be able to love. This was a shattering piece of news. It meant that there was no possibility for me, ever, of getting past 'Go'. My life seemed to bear out the truth of this idea. I had never formed a really close relationship and I felt that I never would, simply because I didn't know how to.

How Can I Love?

This was the burning question I wanted to explore with my Counsellor: how can I love, when I don't feel I have been loved? She was counselling from a Christian model which said that there was an answer to this. Wonderful. My problem had a solution.

'It works like this', she said. 'God loves you, so that means you have some love to give your mother. When you have given your mother some love, she will have some to give you.'

And 'Bingo' everything will be alright? It didn't have the ring of truth to me. In fact it sounded a bit like playing Pass the Parcel. There would, undoubtedly, be something that was being called 'love' going around between us; but would it make me feel that she was loving me? Quite honestly, I didn't think it would.

If it was my love that I was receiving back from her, wouldn't it feel more as though she had simply put a 'Return to Sender' label on the parcel? Further, I didn't think I could just flick a switch in my mind which would change me from thinking she didn't love me to thinking that she did. I could not persuade myself that it was that easy.

There did, however, seem to be two helpful ideas in the Pass the Parcel Model. One was that love somehow moves and involves people. The other was that someone has to start it. For my Counsellor this meant the movement of 'giving' and 'receiving' love between one person and another. This she called the 'flow of love'.

'What', I wondered, 'happens to the flow if one person does not want to receive the parcel they are given? They wouldn't, then, have it to hand back. Alternatively, if they did receive it, they might not want to let it go and so would not return it'. Either way, the flow would stop, like water backed up behind a dam. Nonetheless, the general idea that love is about movement sounded promising.

The second, and even more significant idea for the solution of my problem, was that someone had to start the movement. In my counsellor's rather convoluted thinking it was God who was the initiator. But what if I could start it all off? Could I take the initiative to begin the movement? The psychologists might be wrong; maybe I did not have to wait to be loved by my mother, or anyone else for that matter, before I could love. This was a big idea. It proved to be a key concept in all my subsequent thinking about how loving is done.

If I can take the initiative, I can choose to love. That means love can be can be willed by the lover - by which I mean 'the one who loves', not the one who 'has sex'.

I was getting somewhere. I wrote three statements on a piece of paper:

Love is a movement.
Love is a movement, to do with people.
Love is a movement, to do with people, chosen by the lover.

All I had to do now was to find out was 'what is this thing called love?' and I would be home and dry.

I am a visual person and I very often think with a pencil in my hand. I doodled two pin people; a lover and a beloved: the one who loves and the one who is loved.

That was a start, but if love is to do with movement what sort of movement was I looking for? I drew arrows going from each to the other and looked at it.

I seemed to have two disconnected movements, going in opposite directions. That seemed to illustrate the Pass the Parcel Model which wasn't what I wanted and, seeing it on paper, it looked a bit aggressive; as though they were about to bop each other.

I wondered if there was another way of doing it.

Flow is a continuous movement so either it goes on in roughly the same direction, in which case it would continue on past the intended beloved; or, it runs in some sort of loop like the water in a central heating system. I drew a loop starting from the one who loves, around the one who is loved, and back to the lover.

That looked better. There seemed to be a 'together-ness' about it. As I pondered my doodle I realized another highly significant aspect of this notion of flow. The lover was responsible for the whole of it: both the movement out and the movement back. It was one continuous flow, coming from and returning to the same place.

If this was right, then I, a would-be-lover, really could love on my own initiative, without having to have been loved first. Not only that, I was not dependent on my intended beloved for anything coming back: I could do both the 'giving' and the 'receiving'.

Furthermore, the element of willing, or choosing, to start seemed to suggest something more energetic, more dynamic, than just going with the flow. I looked up the word 'dynamics' in a dictionary and found: 'the motive forces, physical or moral, affecting behaviour and change, in any sphere'. 'Forces affecting behaviour' exactly described the willing behind my notion of loving on my own initiative. I started to think in terms of the dynamic flow of loving.

When I got this far I felt pleased that I appeared to have worked out the mechanics of the flow of love, and its motive power. In a very rudimentary way I had answered my question: 'How do we do it?' But I had skipped over the fundamental one which I was still thinking of as: 'What is this thing called love'?

What Is This Thing Called Love?

One day, when I was pondering the knotty problem of 'what is this thing called love'? a penny dropped with a resounding clunk: 'love is not a thing'. I was asking the wrong question. The flaw of the Pass the Parcel Model is that love is being thought of as an object which can be passed from hand to hand - given and received. Love is not a thing. There isn't a thing called love, separate from ourselves like a parcel. In loving what is given is ourselves and what is received is the other person. And it happens because we choose to give our very selves to our intended beloved, and to receive her or him into ourselves. The loving is the doing of giving ourselves and receiving the person we want to love. That's what love is.

I went back to my three statements about love:

Love is a movement.
Love is a movement, to do with people.
Love is a movement, to do with people, chosen by the lover.

I could now add the finishing touch which answers the question: 'What is [this thing called] love?' It is not a thing at all.

Love is the willed movement of giving ourselves and receiving the other person.

Various new ideas came tumbling out in the wake of this break-through.

Love Is a Verb
Firstly love is something we do; a verb, not a thing, which is a noun. From then on I always referred to this mysterious dynamic flow as 'loving' rather than 'love', to make sure that I did not get confused between a thing and an action.

Anyone Can Start It
Secondly, if loving is something that is done, then this confirmed the possibility that anyone can choose to take the initiative and do it. That meant it was something I could do. I did not have to have felt loved first. I am a DIY enthusiast chiefly, I suspect, because I was born in the wilds of what is now Tanzania, where the culture was: 'If you want it; you make it'. Clothes, jam, amusements, furniture, road bridges were all subject to this rule. The thought that I could start loving, without needing input from anyone else, was huge. It gave me a sense of power, of being in control of my life, which I had never felt before. I could make it happen. All by myself.

Not Dependent on Being Returned
Thirdly, it did not seem that it is a necessary part of the flow of loving that the beloved should pass the parcel back. It is the lover's energy that creates the complete flow in both directions – out and back: and this all solely because he or she had chosen to do it. The lover is not dependent on being loved in order to be

able to love.

The Pass the Parcel Model relies on 'I give you some; you give me some'. If the other person does not want to join in, the game can't be played. The would-be lover is prevented from loving if the intended beloved does not want to love in return. That is what I had believed and yet we know that people do engage in unreciprocated loving. How much of world literature and music is about unrequited love? How much of world morality is about loving those who don't love us, who are our enemies?

The possibility of loving without having to be loved back was highly significant for me because my unloved state had appeared to be an absolute bar to my ever being able to love. The thought that I could love someone, even if they did not love me, opened whole new horizons of possibility for me. I was not, as I had thought, condemned for ever, to being unloving, just because I felt unloved. I shook my head in amazement. I could loop myself around another person, and draw them close to me. I could do a one-lover loving. And I could do it simply because I chose to.

The possibility of loving without being loved in return is one of the glories of the GO-BI loving idea but it is also its chief stumbling block. We all want to be loved and loving without being loved simply does not appear to make sense – until we think about it.

Loving Starts Inside Ourselves

I realized that I would 'only' be doing one-lover loving in my inside self, but I was also dimly aware that it was primarily my inside self that felt so desperately unloved and lonely. I did meet people and do things with them but that did not seem to touch the pain and emptiness inside. At some level I knew, even then, that the fact that I was short of friends in my outside world, had to do with my sense of emptiness on the inside. Friendless-ness was an effect of how I felt about myself rather than a cause.

These were stunning revelations. My mind whirled and my

heart sang: 'I can do it'. 'I can love; all by myself'. 'I don't have to wait to be loved'. I had always believed that no one would be bothered to do anything for me. If I wanted something done, I would have to do it myself. Now I was beginning to think that I could even do loving for myself.

Objections to My Idea

As I began to share my understanding of loving, slight as yet, with other people, two points were always queried. Firstly my contention that it all happens in our inside world - to begin with, at least - and secondly that the non-reciprocal loving I was proposing could not really be loving at all, or, if it was, it could only be second best. Neither of these points was easy to refute; partly due to the fact that, as I was still working on the idea, there were similar doubts lurking in myself. Could what I seemed to have found out really be true?

Inside Loving

We make our decisions inside ourselves and, as loving is a decision, it must at least start happening inside ourselves. This made me feel on fairly firm ground in asserting that the giving of ourselves and the receiving of the other person initially happens in our heads and hearts: it may later find expression outside ourselves.

The idea of an inside and an outside world is helpful in under-standing GO-BI loving and is neatly put by Frederick Buechner in *Telling the Truth*. He says that we carry within us people who may be distant from us in time and place: 'because you do not just live in a world, but a world lives in you'. We have our intended beloved living in us, ready to be looped, if we so desire.

If our beloved is to be made aware of our loving, then, but only then, does it have to be made manifest in our outside world. There could, however, be many reasons why we might choose not to show our loving. We might feel it was inappropriate and be ashamed of it, or we might be afraid our beloved would reject us which would hurt. We can easily be scared away from expressing our loving in our outside worlds.

Loving Doesn't Have To Be Reciprocated

The idea that loving is not dependent on being reciprocated in our outside worlds is much harder to grasp because we do want to feel loving arms around us, not just have them as an idea in our heads. We do want to be loved. However, I clung to my own acute need for a starting place as the rationale for one-lover loving. Later, as I came to understand my model better, I recognized that two people can be loving each other simultaneously which means that as each lover is loving they are also being loved. However, their mutual loving is made up of their own two one-lover GO-BI loving loops. The degree to which each is able to give themselves and receive the other will vary, so their loving will be mutual but it may not necessarily be equal. This is so obviously true, that it satisfied my thinking for the time being.

I experienced a good deal of resistance to the idea that loving doesn't have to be a two-way thing. When we desperately want to be loved it is very hard to get hold of the idea of a loving that is not dependent on someone else. There is, deep within most of us, a longing to know that we are loved because this tells us that, if we make a similar move, we will not be rejected. Without this reassurance we don't have the courage to take the initiative and do our own loving.

There is also often an unconscious quid pro quo to our loving: 'I will love you so that you will love me'. This line of reasoning can get extended into: 'So, if you're not loving me, what's the point in me loving you?' It doesn't get me what I want.

Even if we are not struggling with the fear of being rejected, or with the need to know we are loved, we may still think that it is simply not possible to love someone who does not love us. It may be part of our belief system that loving has got to be mutual.

When we think in any of these ways we cannot experience that GO-BI loving is its own joy and fulfilment; independent of the person we are loving.

Giving and Receiving

The necessary refinements to my raw understanding that would provide more satisfactory, but no less difficult, answers to these objections, were still some years down the road. What did seem important, at this stage of working out the GO-BI loving model, was to come to a better understanding of 'giving' and 'receiving'; both words carried over from the original Pass the Parcel Model.

I had realized that the giving and receiving were about people, not things. I now needed to ask: 'How, exactly, do we give ourselves to, and receive, another?' The giving of the lover must be self-giving - that, when it comes down to it, is all we ever have to give. We may give things - gifts - as tokens, or symbols, of our loving, but the real loving, the real gift, has to be the giving of ourselves.

That thought about giving satisfied me for the time being, so I turned my attention to 'receiving'. I found the word unsatisfactory because it implied taking something that was being handed to us, which was altogether too close to the 'give some; get some' of the Pass the Parcel Model. I seriously wanted to get away from that interdependence because the whole beauty of the loop, for me, was that it was solely the lover's will and energy that made it happen.

Looking at my original doodle, the top one on the cover, I saw that what the loop was doing was a little like lassoing. It was going round the beloved, and drawing or pulling, him or her towards the lover. That was nearer to what I wanted to say, but I wondered if 'pulling' sounded a bit aggressive. A picture came into my head of an unfortunate cow in a Western, with a rope round her neck, being hauled in by a cowboy so she could be branded with a hot iron to show who she belonged to. I have

13

experienced 'love' that felt like being possessed and that was definitely not the loving I was thinking about.

I wanted a word that would give the sense of the beloved being borne in on the flow of the lover's energy. Borne in? A bit random. Brought in? That sounded more purposive; I felt it would do.

So when I was loving I would be giving myself and bringing in my beloved. That was OK but it did not have much of a rhythm to it. 'Bringing in' I liked; so how about 'going out' for giving myself. Thus I arrived at phrases to represent the two movements in the flow of loving; Going Out and Bringing In. They became the acronym GO-BI. The association with the Gobi desert may seem unfortunate, but it is a warning that the road to learning to love in this way can, at times, feel isolated, hard, and barren. I decided to stick with the acronym but to link it with loving. GO-BI loving became the usual form.

That was fifteen years ago. The more I have since thought about the GO-BI loving model as a way of understanding loving, and learned to practice it, the more profound I have realized the two movements of Going Out and Bringing In to be. They can be anything from a simple self-giving and accepting the other, to an ecstatic mystical experience.

The Last Stage

It was not long before I realized that the flow of Going Out and Bringing In was unlikely to be a smooth and continuous one. There were bound to be blocks, holdings-back, keepings-away. The solid line I used in my original doodle was misleading, so I replaced it with a broken one.

Later still I gave the two figures colours, blue and green, which became their names. The little Green person and the little Blue person were born, as the basic GO-BI loving doodle that appears on the cover of this book.

When I started using the doodles on my white board with

people who were interested in the idea the little Green person usually represented the person I was talking with and the little Blue person their intended beloved. This naturally gave them their genders. However, when I came to write about the little Green person and the little Blue person it was very cumbersome not to use pronouns. Short of calling them both 'it' or 'its', which was against all my principles of GO-BI loving, I had to assign genders to them. As the little Green person is usually the initiator I wrestled with issues of sexual equality. However, I found I couldn't keep track of using 'him' and 'her' alternately and, as I couldn't think of anything else, I gave up the struggle and made an arbitrary decision: Green should be female and Blue male. This is purely a stylistic device. It does not say anything about the ability of men or women to initiate GO-BI loving. Nor does it mean that we can only GO-BI love people of the opposite gender. Men can GO-BI love men and women can GO-BI love women.

I felt I had the GO-BI loving model sketched out. What I now needed to do was to think more deeply about what we are actually doing when we are Going Out and Bringing In.

Chapter 2

Going Out and Bringing In

How Going Out and Bringing In Feel

What are we doing when we are GO-BI loving? What does it feel like to be Going Out from ourselves or Bringing In someone, deep into ourselves? These movements start inside ourselves but it is often easier to look at their outward manifestations and then to work out what is happening on the inside.

I was at a funeral some months ago. We were all milling about in the churchyard, after the burial, talking to each other. I noticed people going up to one of the nephews of the person who had died, talk to him for a bit, and then drift away. Now he was standing on his own so I went up to him. I suppose my intention had been to say the usual sympathetic things, but I must have seen a stricken look in his eyes because, when I got up to him, though I am not an indiscriminate hugger, I found myself putting my arms around him. After a moment he started to sob convulsively on my shoulder. I held him.

In that moment I forgot about myself; I was solely aware of his pain – without knowing exactly what it was, but that didn't matter. It was only when he drew away that I became aware of other people again, and consciously put myself between him and them, to give him a bit of privacy in which to recover. What I had been doing and feeling was Going Out. It had started in my inside world with the decision to go over to him and to put my arms around him. The feeling was an emptying of me in order to be intensely with him.

A family Christmas gave me a lovely picture of Bringing In. It was the year that my younger nephew, Paul, was three. He had requested 'a holding bear' for a present. I was offered this

16

commission by my sister-in-law. Neither of us knew what 'a holding bear' was, and though Paul was very clear that that was what he wanted, he couldn't give us any more of a description. I scoured the toy shops but, of the many charming bears I found, none seemed to me to have a quality of 'holding' about them. Eventually I came across a pair of monkeys with long arms and 'Velcro' on their paws so that they could hug each other. As soon as I saw them I knew they had what Paul meant by 'holding'. On Christmas morning, as soon as he had torn the paper off the parcel, he clasped the monkeys to his chest, scuttled out of the room and was not seen again for several hours. There was no doubt in my mind that what I had seen was a Bringing In of those monkeys, deeply in to himself. They were certainly hard to detach when they needed to go to the wash.

Going Out - Giving Ourselves

Going Out is about self-giving or self-offering. The snag with both these terms is that they often carry a connotation of self-sacrifice, which usually has the meaning of wiping ourselves out in favour of someone else. This denies the very existence of our self, which leaves us without a self to give. It is not at all what I mean by self-giving.

The heart of self-giving, Going Out, lies in the way we see the other person. It is not denying ourselves, but focusing all that we are on our beloved, because she is our beloved. In its highest form it is the ecstasy of abandonment to the beloved, when we cease to exist for ourselves. Yet, paradoxically, that is when our real self is most intensely present. Going Out is the melted heart, the all that she is, that flows from a thankful mother to her new born baby. It is the energy behind the phrase 'My heart went out to him', most often used in the face of tragedies where there is nothing to be done. There is a forgetfulness of self in the total attention given to the other, but this does not wipe out the self. It is our quintessential self that is giving the attention. This is why,

I believe, that loving is a spiritual activity – and this applies whether we subscribe to a particular faith or none. It is because loving at its deepest level, where we become one with another, takes us beyond ourselves to ... I don't know where. St. John of the Cross captured this abandonment and forgetfulness of self when he described meeting with his beloved in *The Dark Night* [the Kavanaugh and Rodriguez translation]

> I abandoned and forgot myself,
> Laying my face on my beloved;
> All things ceased; I went out from myself,

Whatever the level of our self-giving, a quick pat on the arm or a significant hug, it can be risky, especially if our life experience has taught us to expect that our offerings will be rubbished, rejected, or ignored. Self-giving at any level can be costly. If we are afraid of what might happen to us when we give ourselves, we may very well decide not to do it. This may be an unconscious decision or a conscious one, but either way, it will deter us from giving ourselves in the first movement of the flow of GO-BI loving.

The First Turn

Once we have chosen to Go Out, there is a moment when we have to decide to turn and make the return movement of Bringing In. Neither Going Out nor Bringing In, on their own, constitute GO-BI loving. Self-giving alone can feel like a hand-out. It is not seeing me as a person. Bringing, or taking in, alone can feel like being possessed: again without regard for me as a person. For our GO-BI loving to be complete we must be engaged in both movements. They are linked by the decision to change the direction of the flow: the First Turn. This is indispensable to the whole idea of GO-BI loving as it prevents the energy of our Going Out disappearing past our intended beloved into the great blue yonder and never coming back. The First Turn starts the movement of bearing our beloved in to us or, to go back to the central heating image, the water in the radiators flowing back to the boiler to be re-heated.

Bringing In – Receiving Others

'Embracing' or 'hugging to ourselves' describes the feeling of Bringing In. I also like the image of sniffing a scented flower. We draw the scent deep into ourselves and it seems to pervade the whole of us. We feel as if the scent has become a living part of ourselves, filling a bit of us that was empty before. There is a sense of fullness or fulfilled-ness about Bringing In. It changes us because we have added something to ourselves. By Bringing In we become a bigger person with more of a self to give.

It also feels scary because we have a greater sense of exposing ourselves. It can be like opening the door to a friend and saying: 'Do come in', knowing that the living room is a tip and that we haven't made the beds or done last night's washing up. If they are a friend who we know accepts us as we are we clear a space for them to sit down and offer them coffee. If we are not quite so sure of them we will try to steer them away from the worst of the mess or, perhaps, if it's really bad, make an excuse and not let them in at all. We simply cannot bear for them to see parts of our lives that we are ashamed of.

Bringing In, like Going Out, can be costly and I have found it the more difficult of the two movements of the flow of loving. Largely this is because when I was a child I felt that my mother owned me. I followed, like a pet dog, where ever she went around the house or on the farm in Tanzania where I was born. I was seven before I spent any of the 24 hours of a day apart from her. It was then that my father returned from the war so I moved out of my mother's bedroom into one of my own. In the afternoons, colonial style, she had a two hour rest. After I had done my piano practice, which she could hear, I was free to do whatever I liked in the fantasy world I created. I felt it was the only time I, myself, lived. When I started thinking about Bringing In it meant opening myself to that sort of possession and it scared me. That was my particular terror but many people have similar fears about Bringing In. We can never be wholly sure what it is going to be like having someone as part of ourselves.

The Second Turn

The first three movements of GO-BI loving: Going Out, the First Turn, and Bringing In establish the principle. They also bring up all the fears we have about making these choices. If we have had a bad time in Going Out or in making the First Turn or in Bringing In, we may decide that the whole process is not worth the candle, and give up. Learning to love is about learning to face our fears, to accept what is, to let go of dreams of how we think it should be, and to forgive our hurts. When we are on the way to doing any, or all, of that we will be free to take the risk, not only of Going Out and Bringing In, but also to make a Second Turn and do it all over again. It is the experience of GO-BI lovers that with time and many Second Turns, our loving gets fuller and richer, because we are Going Out with more of our beloved as well as more of ourselves. We are, in a sense, giving our beloved back to themselves; in the words of Carter Heyward, we are 'loving them into being' and this is a very creative and healing experience for ourselves as well as for them.

Going Out and Bringing In Together Make Loving

Self-giving, on its own, is not GO-BI loving. Receiving another person, on its own, is not GO-BI loving. We need to be doing both in order to be GO-BI loving. The wonderful thing is that, having chosen to love, the Going Out, the First Turn and the Bringing In become one single dynamic. I did not merely Go Out to the man at the funeral; I was also Bringing him In, in the sense that I was holding him and absorbing some of his anguish. Having felt, in my inside world, a desire to Go Out, I forgot all the fears that might have made me hesitate to make the move in my outside world: 'What would other people think'?; 'How ghastly will I feel if he pushes me away?'; 'Will I make things worse for him and then feel horribly guilty?'. Similar fears would have applied to Bringing In, if I had thought about it. 'Do I want this strange man as part of me?'; 'What if he gets attached and wants more of me than I want to give?'; 'What if he sees that part of me that is afraid of men?'; all very good reasons for not GO-BI loving, but when we do decide to Go Out and to Bring In they don't matter anymore. I love the lines in T.S. Eliot's *East Coker*:

> Love is most nearly itself
> When here and now cease to matter.

By the time of the funeral I had, to some extent, come into that freedom but such fears had often prevented me in the past. This is why it is a good idea to think of the loop of GO-BI loving as a broken line: there will always be gaps or stoppages in our flow of Going Out and Bringing In. That I didn't even think of my fears at the funeral was due to the fact that I had already committed myself to the flow of GO-BI loving. I was on my way Out and making the First Turn before I knew it, so Bringing In was simply the same energy coming back into myself. I had completed the loop but that did not mean it was a solid line: my fears were real, but on that occasion, my will to love over-rode them.

The Need To Be Loving
By this stage in my thinking I was satisfied that Going Out and Bringing In were what I had to do if I wanted to be loving. That still left: 'How am I going to get to feel loved? Surely the only way to *feel* loved is by *being* loved?' My heart sank and I felt sick. I knew that however much I said that I wanted to love, - 'and I

do' a little voice inside me squeaked - my deepest longing was to feel loved. If the GO-BI loving model did not have an answer for that then it was not worth the whiteboard it was doodled on.

For some days I sat in the black pit, feeling my whole idea had crumbled around me. Then the first glimmer of light came to me:

'I can't feel loved unless I open myself up to receiving the loving I want by Bringing In the person who is loving me. Alternatively, I can't Bring In someone else's loving, until I am Bringing In the person who is doing the loving. The loving and the lover are all one package'.

So...

'To feel loved I need to be Bringing In the person who is loving me.'

But...

'To Bring In I need first to Go Out, because loving is a single flow'.

Therefore...

'I need to be loving in order to feel loved.' Q.E.D.

Could this really be so? I thought through the implications: supposing the little Blue person was loving the little Green person but she – Green - was not loving him. In doodle terms, the little Green person would have a blue loop going right around her but she might not even notice it was there. She would not feel loved because his loving was not becoming a part of her; it was merely going round her outside. The only way she could make Blue a part of herself, and so feel his loving, would be by

Bringing him In, together with his loving, deep into herself. [The middle doodle on the cover shows Blue deep inside Green.] But, in order to Bring In, she would first have to Go Out. She would have to bite the bullet, take the initiative, and GO-BI love, both Going Out and Bringing In, before she could feel loved.

So it is true. I do need to be loving in order to feel loved.

I know a couple, David and Catherine. He is devoted to her but she is often very sharp with him and complains that he does not care about her. I don't think she is loving him so she doesn't feel his love for her. She won't feel better until she can choose to love David and so Bring him In to herself, together with his loving of her.

I have experienced something like this in my relationship with my cousin Tom. We knew each other as children but did not meet again until eleven years ago. By then he was a happily married father of four with a regular commitment to visit an elderly aunt in the West Country every three weeks. As I lived more or less on the way, he developed the habit of stopping off for breakfast with me. These visits were revelatory because, for the first time in my life, I was talking with someone who took my ideas seriously. We talked, and doodled on the kitchen table. It is to him that I owe the acronym GO-BI.

In time Tom and I created a deep relationship. He was Going Out to me and Bringing me In but, like the little Green person in the example above, I did not feel loved. He said he loved me but I simply did not believe it. In spite of my theorizing, I was still stuck in the place where I believed myself to be unlovable. I felt this simply could not be happening. However, I did now know that I had a choice; I could Go Out and Bring In if I chose to. Choices are funny things. They ought to feel liberating; - 'I'm in control: I have a choice' – but when it comes down to it they are often rather frightening. I battled with my fears of rejection: I simply could not bear to be kicked in the teeth again; my sense of worthlessness; who would want to love me anyway; and my

23

fixed belief that Tom's loving simply could not be. I felt I was Going Out to him but I was not really Bringing him In – the riskier of the two movements.

One day I was writing a letter to him. I can see it now: I was at the right hand side of the page, about four or five lines down from the top when everything stopped – including my breathing I think - and I felt a sensation of Tom flowing in to me. I knew of a certainty that, at last, I had Brought him In; that he was part of me; and I felt loved. We had created a Mutual GO-BI loving. Each of us felt loved because we were Bringing In the other, together with each other's loving. Neither of us would have felt loved if we were only being loved. We had to be loving in order to feel loved.

When I had recovered from the shock, I also knew that the GO-BI loving model was right: it is only in loving that we can feel loved. I know it sounds counter-intuitive: we think we need to be being loved before we feel loved. Nevertheless I believe it does work the other way round. This breathtaking fact is true: we need to be loving in order to feel loved. And we can choose to love any time we want.

When I originally had the idea that we have to be loving in order to feel loved I thought it was new. It's not. I have since discovered that the twelfth century mystic and writer Catherine of Siena said in a letter to Regina della Scala: 'Love is had only by loving'. It couldn't be plainer than that.

One-Lover Loving

The idea that we have to be loving: Bringing In our beloved and his or her loving, in order to feel loved was so exciting that I failed to notice that I had been assuming two people loving each other. I felt drenched in ice cold water as I thought: 'What happens if the person I am Bringing In does not love me? What do I feel then?'

'I can't feel loved if I am not Bringing In someone's love, can

I?' Oops! That thinking was taking me back to the Pass the Parcel Model: 'I give you some, you give me some.' Where had I gone wrong?

Maybe I needed to go back to Paul and his hugging monkeys. Bringing In those cuddly toys certainly did something special for him. He had taken them deep into himself and he obviously felt good about having them there. I did the doodle of the little Green person with the little Blue person as part of herself because she had Gone Out and Brought him In and asked myself: 'What does it feel like to have someone I really love nestling inside me?' It feels warm. There's a mixture of wonder and pleasure: 'Is this really happening? Can I really melt into my beloved and he into me?' I think some sort of deep togetherness was going on between Paul and his monkeys. They were stuffed toys so they could not be loving him back. He was one-lover GO-BI loving.

If one-lover loving feels that good, if it gives us the sense of being filled with our beloved, is it that different from how it feels to be loved? Part of me said: 'Don't be ridiculous. Being loved is different so it must feel different.'

Another part chipped in: 'Yes but... I feel loved because I am Bringing In: because I am GO-BI loving. It is having my beloved as part of myself that gives me the dizzy, warm feeling.' In that sense loving does feel the same as being loved. This is the other breathtaking fact about GO-BI loving: one-lover loving can give us the same feeling that being loved does.

Filling The Void

Most of us, at some time in our lives, have been aware of a void, an emptiness, in the very depths of ourselves. This void is caused by the knowledge that something that should be there, isn't. We think of the void as an I-want-to-be-loved shaped hole and we tend to believe that this space can only be filled by the person who we want to be loved by. When that doesn't happen we use chocolate, work, alcohol, or even another person, as fillers instead. The glory of GO-BI loving is in showing us that it doesn't have to be that way. We don't have to go on feeling empty, we don't have to wait to be loved: there is something we can do about it right now. By one-lover GO-BI loving the person whose loving we long for, we can bring them into our I-want-to-be-loved shaped void and feel that it is filled. It took a lot of staring at the middle doodle on the cover before I could really take this astounding fact on board.

The End of My Search

My search for an understanding of how can I love had arisen out of the belief that if I had not been loved then I would never be able to love. Through working with my doodles, for myself and other people, I had decided that this was not true. I now knew that I could choose to love; that I would have to be loving in order to feel loved; and that loving could give me the same feeling as being loved.

There was, however, one thing that still needed thinking about. Had I lost out by not feeling loved, and if so, was there anything I could do about it at this late stage in my life. The next thing to be considered, therefore, was: 'What does being loved do for us?'

Chapter 3

Being Loved

What Does Being Loved Do For Us?

The first thing we need if we are to Go Out in self-giving is a self to give. That sounds blindingly obvious but try to answer the question: 'Who am I?' without saying 'a manager, a spouse, a member of the sports club,' and most of us get a bit stuck. We need a sense of our own identity in order to start GO-BI loving. In addition to identity we need a sense of security within ourselves if we are to GO-BI love. We have to feel: 'It's OK to be me', and to be reasonably sure that the world is an OK place. If we learn that even when we have bad experiences someone will pick us up and dust us down we learn that we can cope. Without a trust that all ultimately will be well, very few of us have the courage to take the initiative to start GO-BI loving.

I have some friends, Rob and Jane, who have a small son, Thomas. They love Thomas. Right from the beginning they delighted in him: they smiled at him and talked to him and called him their special boy; they looked into his eyes and really saw him. From that he learned who he was. Even when he got bigger and had to learn the meaning of 'No' it was always said in such a way that he knew that it was his behaviour that was wrong, not his very self. From that he has learned that it is OK to be him, even when he is making Mummy cross. That, I think, makes him feel deep down safe. He has also learned to feel physically safe because from the beginning he was held by both Jane and Rob; he could always go to them if he hurt himself; and, if he called out in the night, one of them would always come. He knows he matters. Because he knows who he is; he is Thomas, Mummy and Daddy's special boy, and because he feels safe to be him and to be in the world where he lives, he is able to trust people. He is a very friendly little boy.

As he grows older he will discover that the world is not always a friendly place but he will also find that he can cope because his personality is built on the firm foundations of identity, security and trust. He feels safe enough to give himself and to be open to receiving other people. He has learned to GO-BI love without even knowing it. His parents' loving has given him that gift.

When we have been loved as children we grow up with a view of the world as a generally friendly place, a place in which it is safe, even natural, to Go Out and to Bring In. The good news is that even if we have missed out on this foundation of being loved as children the same thing can happen if we are loved as adults, perhaps for the first time. But it will be a long, hard journey because there will be lots of fears and insecurities to be unlearned first.

From Wanting to Loving

Being loved tells us who we are and that the world is, by and large, a safe place, in which we can trust that all will be well enough. It is no wonder that our heart's cry is 'I want to be loved.' It seems to be the solution to most of the problems of living and loving.

Being loved calls us into being. Our personality blossoms when we are loved. Without love our growth is stunted, we shrivel and a part of us dies. We don't know who we are and we don't trust that anybody will keep us safe. This is what happens to people who have been abused, whether it be physically, sexually, emotionally or spiritually. The perpetrator denies the victim's personhood, in effect saying: 'I and my needs are more important than you. You don't matter. You are nobody'. When we don't seem to impact anyone else's life; when we are ignored, we feel we cease to exist, or, perhaps, that we should not exist. I have stood on a railway bridge thinking just that.

Alternatively we may think that if we only exist to satisfy another's need, our survival depends on being what that other wants us to be. In that case being who we really are could be dangerous. We will be afraid to be ourselves and will not want to trust ourselves to, give ourselves to, anyone. Without the identity, security and trust which we get from being loved, we tend to think that anyone and everyone is a potential threat, and that the whole world is against us.

If we are already wobbly in our sense of identity, security and trust, we gaze longingly at those we feel are loved and think that, if only we were like that, all would be well. The trouble is that once our sense of self has been sufficiently damaged we cease to believe that we can be loved; we come to believe that we are not lovable.

The word 'lovable' is usually taken to mean 'able to be loved'. If people find us lovable it means that they can love us. It could also be rendered 'love-able' meaning 'able to love'. The desperate cry of the person who feels unloved: 'I want to be lovable', can, by an act of will, be turned into a declaration of hope: 'I want to be able to love'. This is the message of GO-BI loving.

If we make this change in our thinking, we can turn our world upside down and inside out. The whole emphasis has shifted. Suddenly we are in charge. Instead of longing, helplessly, for somebody to do something, we can take the initiative. This is not easy if we have a damaged sense of self, if we do not feel we have a self to Go-Out with. If we don't feel safe and cannot trust, it is very hard to dare to Bring-In. But once we have decided to say: 'I want to love' in place of 'I want to be loved', we have taken our life into our own hands instead of leaving it a hostage to others.

Loving Ourselves

The wonderful thing is that the very act of saying: 'I want to love' gives us an identity: 'I am a person who wants to love'. That is

29

who I am. I don't necessarily have to have learned it from other people; I can teach it to myself. I can also be seen by myself. One of the most powerful exercises in recognizing our selves is to look into our own eyes in a mirror: to 'see' ourselves. It took me ages to be able to do it.

When we have chosen to give ourselves an identity, have looked into our own eyes and said: 'I see you', we begin to feel it is OK to be ourselves: it starts to feel safe. This is because no one can take away what we have given ourselves – except, of course, ourselves. We will occasionally lose our sense of ourselves and then we will, temporarily, tumble back into the black pit, but it gets increasingly easy to climb back out. Having a self-given identity, and feeling that it's OK to be us, we are in a better position to trust that we can handle whatever we find in the world around us. What we have done is to GO-BI love ourselves. If we think in terms of the GO-BI loving doodles, we are, at once, both the little Green person and the little Blue person. The Green Us – the one that did the seeing - is Going Out to Blue Us – the us we have 'seen' - and is Bringing In that second us, making us feel complete and safe because we are loved – by us. Again a good, long stare at the middle doodle on the cover helps give reality to this daft sounding proposition, that I can GO-BI love myself and give myself, if nobody else has, the benefits of being loved.

Somewhere along the GO-BI loving road, I realized that I was not loving myself. I had felt utterly and irrevocably unlovable for most of my life. I blamed 'the world' for this state of affairs; I was not loved so that was why I felt unlovable. I now saw that there were things about me, my body, my inability to relate to people, and my stupidity, that I hated. And because there were things about me that I hated, I hated me.

Being able to GO-BI love other people and GO-BI loving ourselves are intimately connected. When we don't like ourselves, we assume that nobody else is going to like us either, so to Go Out to them is to invite rejection, and to Bring In, apart from being impossible until we are Going Out, is also to risk being hurt in some way. It is frightening to think of giving someone access to our inside world. They may step on some very tender bits of us.

Unless we can love ourselves; get alongside ourselves; accept ourselves as we are, we are not going to be able to love, to get alongside and accept, other people. Also what we don't like in ourselves, we tend to dislike in other people. If there is a lot we don't like about ourselves, there is going to be a lot we don't like in other people which will make Going Out and Bringing In very difficult.

There is another aspect to not liking ourselves: I didn't like myself so I was completely unable to understand that anyone else could like me, or want to be with me. I simply blocked anyone's attempt to show they cared about me and so, not unnaturally, they felt I was pushing them, and their feeling, away. [Which I was]. They felt hurt and backed off. I then felt rejected in my turn. The flow of GO-BI loving could not be established on either side, and all because I could not believe there was anything likable, let alone lovable, about me.

I have come a long way down my own, personal, GO-BI loving road since then, but my external world has not changed all that much. I am still single and I don't have a rip-roaring social life. I have some very good friends; but I am still 'on my own in the world'. However, because I have learned to GO-BI love, I have a deep awareness of belonging to the rest of humanity. I feel connected. Even brief meetings when someone comes to the door, or sympathetically catching the eye of a mother struggling with a recalcitrant child in the High Street, give me an internal glow and a sense of drawing them into myself. I no longer feel achingly lonely. I have learned how to connect deeply with other people.

Sometimes, at bedtime, when I review my day, it dawns on me that I have not had a real conversation with anyone, and yet

31

I feel I have had a full day and I am at peace. I have been alone, but I have not felt lonely. The glory, the excitement, of being in this place can only be appreciated by those of us who have known the bottomless black hole of acute loneliness.

By learning to GO-BI love ourselves we don't have to wait to be loved before we can go and be loving; before we can become love-able people. In our inside world we have started to give ourselves all the benefits of being loved: identity, security and trust and, in turn, these give us a self to give and the courage to take the risk of Going Out and Bringing In.

Chapter 4

Relationship and Loving

Awareness

It takes a long time to learn to GO-BI love ourselves. In the process we get to know ourselves; we become more aware of the self that we are loving. Awareness is about how we engage with our inside worlds; and also with our outside worlds, and the people in them. Awareness is more than merely noticing that we are standing next to someone in the coffee queue. To be aware of someone we have to allow them to impact us. When we have been aware of someone we say: 'He made an impression on me', or 'I was struck by her'.

We have to cultivate the habit of awareness of ourselves, of how we are feeling; what we are thinking, before we can be aware of what is going on around us and how other people are thinking and feeling. I have found that those who are not very self-aware are often not very good at noticing other people or what is happening in their vicinity. This can make for loneliness and isolation.

A while ago I was out with a friend, walking along the edge of a wood. It was summer and different sorts of bumblebees were bumbling in and out of the foxglove bells. I said: 'Oh, look. There's an orange-bummed one' – a Red Tailed Bumblebee to the purists. My friend said, in surprise: 'Do they come in different colours? I'd never noticed'. This was odd since she had been brought up in the country. It was also sad that she had gone through life like Frances Cornford's Fat Lady 'missing so much and so much'. She doesn't notice much about herself either. Deep down she is lonely.

Being aware involves noticing with the whole of ourselves. To do that we have to be aware of our own wholeness: our essential selves who have bodies, emotions, thoughts and spirit to employ in becoming aware of another person.

With our bodies we can see, touch, or hear another person – even smell or taste them if we use all five of our senses.

With our emotions we can feel something about someone; they have significance for us.

With our thoughts we can think something about someone we meet; they have meaning for us.

With our spirit, our imagination and creativity, we can have an intuitive perception about another person.

To be really aware of another person, or even a bumblebee, we need to employ all of these aspects of ourselves.

Capacity for Awareness

Our capacity for awareness of other people depends on our level of awareness of ourselves. We cannot be aware that someone else is sad or angry or afraid if we are never aware of having those emotions in ourselves: if we simply don't know what it feels like to be sad or angry or afraid.

There is a fullness of living that comes from being aware of ourselves, other people and the world in which we live, but it is costly. One of the very first people I counselled was a lady who was depressed. Inexperienced as I was, we were able to do some work which made her more aware of her essential self and she was able to let go of some of the thoughts and feelings which had been deadening her life. Some years later I met her in the street and greeted her with the usual: 'How are you?' 'Fine, thanks,' she replied: 'But sometimes a bit raw. I feel everything so much more now'. She was paying the price, very willingly, for being more aware and engaging herself more fully in the sorrows and joys of her life.

Self awareness, noticing what is going on in our bodies, emotions, thoughts, and spirits helps us to become more aware that we have a self to give, that essential starting point for Going Out and Bringing In, in GO-BI loving. I use a meditation, adapted from a dis-identification exercise devised by Roberto Assagioli, which helps us separate out our essential 'I' from our bodies, emotions, thoughts and spirits. This is how it works: sit quietly and say to yourself: 'I have a body and I am choosing to be aware of my body', then try to notice each little itch, tremor, and ache in your body. Be aware of the weight of your hands in your lap, your thighs touching your chair. After a while say to yourself: 'I have a body and I am not my body'. Repeat the sequence with your emotions, your thoughts, and your spirit, which you may prefer to call your creativity or intuition. Finish each sequence with the affirmation: 'I have... I am not...'. Simply notice what arises; don't try to name everything. When you have spent some time being aware of each aspect of yourself say:

'I am choosing to be aware of I;
I am choosing to be;
I am;
I'.

Most people experience a sense of peace at this moment, as they come home to their true selves; the self they have to give in GO-BI loving.

My Relationship Model

Awareness is also involved in creating relationships. Though we talk of two people being 'in a relationship', meaning that they are more than 'just good friends', relationship and GO-BI loving are two different things. However, they often go together so I want to say something about my model of relationship.

I was counselling Stella who was having difficulties in her marriage. It became important to sort out the difference between GO-BI loving and relationship because she was struggling with both. To have a relationship with someone we have to be aware of them, but do they have to be aware of us? That was the question that Stella was wrestling with. She did not feel that Roger, her husband, was aware of her as a whole person but she was aware of him. This imbalance made her discontented in the marriage. She was angry with him.

How a Relationship Works

A doodle was called for to help her see what makes a relationship and how it works. I drew two pin people, A and B, with arrows pointing towards each other. These represented their awareness of each other which was a two-way thing: one arrow from A pointing towards B for A's awareness of B; another arrow from B representing B's awareness of A.

As I did this doodle I realized that it was oddly reminiscent of my first GO-BI doodle which I rejected on the grounds that it implied two disconnected movements when, at the time, I was wanting to show the idea of a single flow returning to its source. However, in relationship two separate movements is just how it does work: I am aware of you and you are aware of me and our two individual awarenesses create the one relationship. To show this I drew a circle around my two pin people which represented the 'our-relationship' which was made up of the two individual 'my-relationships' or awarenesses each of the other. Both the arrows were the same length showing that the people in the doodle were equally aware of each other. The arrowheads could have been closer to each other or further apart illustrating the degree of closeness in that particular our-relationship. When the arrowheads touch an our-relationship can become a two-way GO-BI loving.

Looking at the relationship doodle I had done, Stella asked: 'But couldn't they be aware of each other without being in the circle together – like at a party? You see him; then he sees you, but by then you've stopped looking at him. Nothing happens until you catch each other's eye, and know that you are looking at each other'.

'That's it.' I said. 'That's the final ingredient. Each has to be aware of the other's awareness before an our-relationship is created.'

Stella pondered the doodle I had done with two equal length arrows representing the our-relationship of herself and Roger. She said: 'I feel our relationship looks more like this' and she leaned forward and wiped away Roger's arrow. According to my Relationship Model this was now no longer a relationship at all because the essential element of mutual awareness was missing.

As we continued to talk and doodle we decided that it was more accurate to show Roger's awareness with a very short arrow because he did say: 'Hello. Had a good day?' when he got back from work, even though he didn't wait for an answer. There was some awareness, but not a lot. Not nearly as much as Stella had of him: she noted how he shut the front door, whether he looked tired, and whether his newspaper was scrunched up which meant that he was in a bad mood.

This led us to consider that the degree of awareness in the two my-relationships that go to make an our-relationship doesn't have to be the same. One person can be more or less aware than the other. This could be shown by a longer or shorter arrow.

The next obvious question was: 'What sort of our-relationship is it when the arrows are of different lengths?' The answer is that the shorter of the two arrows governs the degree of closeness of the whole our-relationship. This is because it is only the shorter length that they have in common; it represents that part of their awareness which is mutual. This can be very hard on the person with the longer arrow because they have some capacity to be aware that the other half of the relationship cannot match.

Stella's Problem

This was Stella's problem: she and Roger had unequal length

arrows in their our-relationship. He was putting less of himself, probably because he was less aware of himself, into their our-relationship than she was. This meant that the amount of mutual awareness, that which they had in common, was only his short arrow length. It also meant that she had some arrow length, or awareness, going spare. So what was Stella to do with the rest of her arrow; her spare capacity to be aware and to engage?

This is where understanding the difference between relationship and GO-BI loving is useful. I did the GO-BI doodles for Stella and explained that Roger did not need to love her for her to decide to love him with her spare capacity – if she chose. She did not so choose. She was angry.

'It's not fair. Why should I love him when he doesn't love me?'

Underneath the relationship problems, was the fact that she didn't feel loved. Now we were getting somewhere. There was a lot of exploring to do to tease out why she felt unloved and a lot of hurt and anger to be brought to the surface before she could come to accept Roger for who he was and to let go of the pain she felt that he was not who she wanted him to be. When she had done that it was not so difficult to Go Out to him with that spare part of herself and to Bring him In to her deepest self, that part of her he could not even imagine was there because he was not aware of anything like it in himself. In short, she found herself GO-BI loving him.

Chapter 5

The GO-BI Loving Road

Rebellion in the Ranks

While I was figuring out how GO-BI loving works and how it can be used to make up for the difference in arrow lengths in an our-relationship I was also trying to put it into practice. A theory that does not actually work on the ground has got to have something wrong with it.

As I tried to Go Out and to Bring In I became aware that when I found I couldn't it was not because the GO-BI loving model was at fault but that there were bits of me that simply did not want to do it. When I had chosen to love: my will, my self said: 'Go for it' but there was rebellion in the ranks of my body, emotions, mind and spirit. One or more of them said: 'That's too risky' or 'You must be joking. Go Out to him?' and I would find myself not able to do what I wanted to do.

This wasn't simply a problem for me. Many of my counsellees had similar sorts of internal dialogue going on inside themselves. We are not always as free as we would like to be to do the things we would like to do.

The 'Shall I? Shan't I?' Debate

Our body, emotions, mind and spirit carry a lot of useful information, stored in their memories, about how to conduct ourselves through life. The trouble is that it is highly conditioned by our previous experience. When we want to do something they will start a 'Shall I? Shan't I?' debate and if our emotions have experienced pain in the past, for instance from being ignored, they will say, when an invitation arrives: 'Don't go to that party.' However, it may be that our mind will say: 'Oh, come on. You will know lots of people. It will be fun' to which our emotions reply: 'Well, I'm not risking it'. We have an impasse. Our mind and body may get us to the party, but if our emotions are still frightened they will keep us stuck in a corner, justifying our expectation of having a miserable time.

The 'Shall I? Shan't I?' debate raises all sorts of questions about the advisability of embarking on Going Out and Bringing In.

Questions About Going Out

Do I Really Want To Go Out?
The Little Green person may, at the moment, have little desire to Go-Out to the little Blue person. They have just had an almighty row and she is thinking: 'Why should I make the first move to repair our relationship?', or 'It was his fault, so he should say sorry first'. When she is feeling like this her anger is an obstacle to her Going Out: she does not want to be anywhere near him. Before she is able to Go-Out to him she is going to have to forgive him; and forgive herself for her part in the row. Forgiving is one of the tools for overcoming obstacles to GO-BI loving.

Do I Dare to Go Out?
The little Green person may not dare to Go-Out to the little Blue person because she is afraid. She has a picture burned on her memory of going up to a likely looking man at a party, and saying something to him. He looked over her shoulder, said: 'I must just catch Sophie', and disappeared. She remembers nearly bursting into tears. She is not going there again.

She may also be afraid to Go Out because she believes she is worthless and she doesn't want anyone to find out how 'nothing' she is. This is probably the biggest single reason why little Green persons don't dare to Go-Out to little Blue persons. She may also not dare to Go-Out to him because she feels guilty about some offence she has, or thinks she has, committed against him. Guilt is a great keeper-away.

She is struggling to surmount two obstacles. One is fear of being rejected and there is a tool for overcoming this: Facing down our Fear. The other is that she is holding deep down beliefs about herself which are not true. There is a way of overcoming these too.

Can I give myself in Going Out?

The little Green person may also find herself wondering: 'Can I give myself to the little Blue person?' This is a different question from: 'Do I want to give myself?' It asks: 'Even if I wanted to, and even if I dared to, is it possible, or practicable, to give myself to anyone else?'

She is right to wonder about this, because she can never know herself completely, so she cannot give the whole of herself to a little Blue person. There will always be deep down recesses of her unconscious mind that she does not know about. What she can do is give as much of herself as she is aware of at any one time, and then give more when she finds more of herself. This has been a major part of my rationale for trying to become more aware of myself. The more I 'have' of me, the more I have to give in my chosen action of loving. We do, of course, have uncon-scious parts of ourselves that we give because they are part of who we are, but they merely come along for the ride. They are not part of the chosen action of Going Out; they can't be because we don't know about them.

There is a similar doubt about Bringing In. 'Can I Bring In all of my intended beloved?' The answer is 'No' for the same reasons. We can't know all of another person but as we grow in awareness, our ability to Bring In will grow too; even to the point of being prepared to Bring In unknown parts of our intended beloved.

Questions About Bringing In

Do I Want To Bring In?

'Do I really want to push the little Blue person away more than I want to Bring him In?' is a classic internal conflict and often has its roots in resentment or disappointment, both of which are related to anger.

We sometimes feel we need to be emotionally or physically close to express anger, but once we get some energy behind our words, or even our fist, the effect is to drive away. Bringing In the little Green person is choosing to have the little Blue person, whom she wants to GO-BI love, right in her inner most being. If she is angry with him, she may want to get to grips with him, but she certainly doesn't want him as part of herself. The tool of Forgiving helps take down the obstacles that disappointment and anger erect along the GO-BI loving road.

Will He or She Hurt Me?

The next two questions: 'Will he hurt me?' and: 'Do I want him close?' can at first sight appear to be much the same, in that fear of someone invading our safety zone is behind them. The difference is that: 'Do I want him close?' is, about the fear of intimacy, whereas 'Will he hurt me?' is about fear of pain; physical or emotional. If the hurt was something like being in hospital and having nurses and doctors do painful things, it is probably a bit easier for the little Green person, in later life, to make sense of it. She knows she was ill when she was three. However, she may still feel a tightening in her guts when she comes in contact with certain people in white coats. Her body will remember the pain and will send a warning signal to her emotions, mind and spirit: 'Watch out! You're about to be hurt'. If the little Blue person she wants to love happens to be a painter who always wears a white smock this could prove a significant obstacle to her efforts to Bring him In, especially if she is not aware of the connection her body is making between white coats and being hurt.

Emotional hurts are often harder to trace to their origins. I have a generalized fear of not being good enough which comes from the pain of feeling that I was never the person Mum wanted me to be. There was a time when, if someone suggested I could do something differently, instead of considering the idea on its merits, I would immediately assume that I was being told that I had got it wrong and feel terribly hurt.

Do I Want Him or Her Close?

If we have been betrayed, perhaps by being sexually abused by someone we trusted, we can be very afraid at the thought of having anyone that close to us again. We will be afraid of intimacy, and yet, we long for closeness. We long to be able to Bring In our special little Blue person; to have him deeply a part of ourselves.

Maybe we do achieve it, one evening when the moon is shining, and it is wonderful, but Bringing In that once can create another hurdle to be got over. At the end of the evening he goes home and we are alone again. We have a moment of panic and think we will never see him again and the pain of that sense of loss may be so excruciating that we decide it is too high a price to pay for the glory of Bringing In. Possibly without realizing it, we put the chain on the door and, henceforth, let no potential lover over our threshold. We have decided that it hurts too much to have someone that close.

Will He or She Take Possession Of Me?

This question also has fear as its bottom line. One of the past experiences that can give rise to it is 'smother love' where a parent's over-protective love inhibits a child's natural impulse to explore and to take risks, leaving him or her afraid to do pretty much anything.

We can also feel 'possessed' when we are being 'lived through' by a parent trying to re-write, in us, the script of his or her own unfulfilled life. We see it in parents who drive a talented child to excel in their particular gift, and don't give them time to do the ordinary things their friends are doing.

When we have experienced this sort of taking-over as a child our body, emotions, mind and spirit put up a strong fight against letting it happen again. If they win we will decide against Bringing In anyone to our inside world.

For a long time I was afraid to Bring In Mum. She did love me passionately, in her own needy way, but I was afraid of being engulfed by her need so I kept her loving out. Choosing to GO-BI love always carries a high risk.

Chapter 6

Different Kinds of Loving

'Authentic' and 'Inauthentic' Love

I had become convinced that the GO-BI loving model was the answer to my original question: 'How can I love?'. I had gone through the phase of grappling with all the questions that the answer threw up; which had brought me back to my relationship with my Mum.

About that time I read *Love's Endeavour, Love's Expense* by W. H. Vanstone. It had made a great impression on me: he talked about 'authentic love' and 'inauthentic love'. Authentic love is the sort that has the beloved's best interests at heart, whereas inauthentic is the sort that meets a need in the lover. It had never occurred to me that loving could be meeting a need in the lover but immediately it made perfect sense. It explained why Mum had always said she loved me and yet I had never felt loved so I blamed myself: I thought I must be unlovable.

However, there always had been a part of me which knew, though I would have been quite incapable of putting it into words, that what Mum was calling 'love' was inauthentic. Mostly she needed my presence to assuage her deep loneliness in Africa. Her love was not for me, as me, the child she might have delighted in. It was an attempt to meet her need for closeness which, I believe, could only have been met by another adult woman: certainly not by me. Later, after we came to England, she did find her need for status met in my occasional successes.

A family wedding gave her such an opportunity. By then I was a professional dress designer, and had made the bride's dress. The guests, as is usual on such occasions, said: 'Doesn't she look a picture?' Mum derived considerable pleasure from telling people that 'my daughter' had made the dress; not 'Jonquil' I noted. I did not feel that particular creation was very successful. However, I had recently master-minded the making of a cope for a retiring Vicar which I felt was the best piece of work I had ever done. I had brought the picture from the local newspaper to show Mum. She was not interested; there was nothing in it for her.

It was out of this confusion that I found the whole idea of different sorts of 'loving' fascinating. What Vanstone had called 'authentic loving' was what I had come to think of as GO-BI loving, but in order to understand my model better I needed to look at non-GO-BI sorts of loving: Vanstone's 'inauthentic loving'.

One of these is 'loving' that treats the beloved as an object from which some satisfaction is gained. There is also a 'loving' that is trying to fill a void inside the lover and a 'loving' that uses the 'beloved' to make the lover feel better about him or her self. Interestingly these kinds of loving are all about getting something for ourselves; they don't make the movement of self giving so they can't Bring In, in GO-BI loving.

A Satisfying Object

An object is an 'It'. Can we GO-BI love an 'It'?. We do say: 'I just love your new sofa' – but are we really talking GO-BI loving? We are happy to look at our friend's new sofa – and that may be a sort of Going Out – but do we really want a sofa as part of our innermost selves? I think not. There is always a sense of standing over against an 'It': we keep it outside ourselves. That is why we can never truly GO-BI love an 'It'.

Objects are things we use: that fulfil a purpose for us. Treating someone as an object makes them feel used and strips them of their personhood. When someone is an object to us we are unaware of them as a person with a body, emotions, mind and spirit. I have a friend who survived her childhood by meeting her own needs however she could. She was going away on holiday and asked if she could borrow a light-weight jacket of mine. I said: 'Sure', and then added: 'but haven't you got a very similar one of your own?' 'Oh yes', she replied: 'but I don't want mine to get spoiled'. She had no idea what she had said: that she had reduced me to an object; a source of expendable jackets. I felt used.

One of the worst ways of being turned into an object is for a child to be sexually abused. The abuser only sees the child as an object with which to satisfy her or his needs. They may say: 'You are my special girl' – or 'boy', but this is only so they can follow it up with: 'And this is our special secret', thereby buying the child's silence. The tragedy is that the child often mistakes this special-ness for the love they crave. When they try to create relationships or GO-BI lovings of their own, they treat other people as objects to meet their needs in the same way that they were treated. It's all they know but it doesn't get them the closeness they long for.

To be turned, emotionally, into an object is one of the most damaging things that can happen to us, especially if it happens when we are young. I can't count the number of times counsellees have said to me things like: 'I felt I was nothing', 'I felt I didn't exist', 'I was a nobody'. I have said them myself and I know the desolate place they come from. We are looking for our essential self to be recognized, because something obscure inside us tells us that we are 'a somebody'. When we are not seen we feel it must be because we are not a person. We know we have physical mass so we assume we must be some sort of object and, very often, we allow ourselves to be used like an object because that seems to be what we deserve.

If we are failing to, or choosing not to, be aware of someone as a whole person we are treating them as an object. If we are seeing a person as an object, we cannot GO-BI love them.

The Hole Inside

I have talked about 'filling the void': the empty space inside many of us, with various things, including a person.

Mary and Russell are married to each other but they are not happy together. Neither of them felt loved by their parents so each of them has a huge parent-shaped hole inside. They want their voids filled and they are looking at each other 'as if' they are the parent whose love they want. This means that neither of them is seeing their partner as the person who they really are. They are treating each other as void-fillers; as objects in place of the parents whose love they crave. They are two children in search of their Mum and Dad. The love they have for each other as a married couple isn't authentic. They are not GO-BI loving each other for who they really are. But it does not have to stay that way. Once they understand what they are doing they will be able to work on letting go of their parents. That will open the way to authentically GO-BI loving each other.

Loving To Feel Better About Ourselves

There is also a 'loving' the primary purpose of which is to make the lover feel better: to give meaning to his or her life. Parents can derive their meaning from their children; spouses from their other halves; carers from the people they look after.

Rita, who had difficulty in conceiving a child, was especially vulnerable to this. She felt she was a failure as a woman because she was not able to do the one thing that women are uniquely programmed to do. When, at last, she gave birth to a little girl, the baby became a symbol telling Rita that she was OK. She did not see baby Alison as a person in her own right.

As Alison grew, Rita became an over-anxious mother, protecting her child from every possible danger. The effect this had on Alison, was to make her clingy and afraid to take risks in playing with other children or to do anything on her own. Finally Rita's behaviour was recognized as a problem and she came to see me. When we unpacked her story, Rita discovered that, dearly as she thought she loved Alison, what she really deeply felt was: 'This child says something to me, about me. She proves I am a proper woman. I'm not a failure any more'. In protecting Alison from all possible danger, she was protecting her own self-image. She was over-careful of Alison because without her child she would lose the good feeling of having made it, at last, into the world of proper women.

Self-focus and Other-focus

Useful as I found W. H. Vanstone's idea of 'authentic' and 'inauthentic' ways of loving I did not like the actual words: they sounded a bit judgmental to me. Thinking, about it one day, I realized that the difference between authentic and inauthentic lay in the direction in which we are looking. When our loving is authentic it is GO-BI loving. Our attention is focused on our beloved. The direction of our gaze is the same as our Going Out flow of loving.

Inauthentic loving is the other way round. We are looking to ourselves first, so we never really Go Out. Even if we do draw the other person into our orbit it is to take from them rather than to Bring them In, in the GO-BI loving sense.

The terms Other-focused and Self-focused seemed to highlight that it is the direction of our attention that distinguishes the two different ways of loving that Vanstone had identified. Either can become our habitual way of being, our default position from which we see, and respond to, the world around us.

The Difference Between Awareness and Focus

Being Self-focused is an obstacle to GO-BI loving but, if we are to have a self to give in Going Out, we need to be self-aware. So what is the difference?

Being self-aware is knowing ourselves, accepting, as far as we can, that we are as we are. Focus is the direction we are facing. Being Self-focused is having our attention on ourselves; feeling driven to look to ourselves and to get our own needs met.

Awareness and focus are not mutually exclusive. We can be very aware of the car approaching the cross-roads on which we have the right of way. Our awareness of the car is as a potential danger to ourselves; it might not stop. We are aware of the other car but, in seeing to our own safety, our focus, will be on ourselves. On the other hand, when my visitor, Gill, takes her muddy boots off before walking across my carpet, she is being self-aware and Other-focused at the same time. She is being aware of her own dirty foot-wear but her attention is focused on my carpet, and, by extension, on me.

Self-focus and GO-BI Loving

We can't be GO-BI loving when we are being Self-focused. It simply can't be done because Self-focus keeps us locked inside ourselves; trying to keep ourselves safe. That is not a position from which we can Go Out. However, sometimes it is difficult to tell the difference between Self-focus and Other-focus. Self-focus, I want to be loved, can lead us to act in a way that looks Other-focused. That causes problems for ourselves and the person on the other end of the action. We do not get the love we want because we are going about it in the wrong way. The person we are 'loving' is subtly aware of the difference between a Self-focused action, designed to get something for ourselves, and an Other-focused one, which is part of an expression of GO-BI loving. They feel used.

I had a counsellee, Margaret, who desperately wanted to be liked, to feel useful; she wanted to be loved. As we began to explore her family background we discovered that her parents mostly ignored her. They only took notice of her if she did a job that pleased them. So she did as many jobs as she could find, hoping to get loved. It didn't work but she kept trying. She was still trying in adulthood. She worked tirelessly for other people but she still did not seem to make friends or to feel loved. Though she did not realize it, she was treating them as objects to satisfy her need for acceptance and love: she was not really Going Out to them so she could not Bring them In, with their love and appreciation, if it was there.

Margaret's deep down motivation, in all her service to other people was to get herself loved. She did not see those she served as whole people. She did not see that they liked her anyway. She could only see them as a source of the love she wanted. When we have just one thing in our sights it is hard, to the point of impossibility, to be aware of the whole of the person who might deliver it to us. We can never Go Out to them, nor Bring them In because we simply don't see them.

It was hard for Margaret, coming from her background, to learn the GO-BI loving lesson that we only feel loved when we are loving.

Other-focus and GO-BI Loving

We can only be Other-focused when we have got to the place where we feel sufficiently secure in ourselves not to have to worry about getting our needs met; not to have to worry about what other people think of us; not to have to worry whether we will get hurt or not. It takes a lot of growing to know that we have a self, an 'I', that is doing OK. When we do, we can be Other-focused and Go Out and Bring In, in GO-BI loving. Interestingly the more we are self-aware, the less self-focused we feel compelled to be.

Dame Julian of Norwich said: 'All shall be well. And all manner of thing shall be well'. It took me a long time to see this as anything more that a pious hope that nothing nasty was going to happen – which I didn't believe. I have now come to understand her saying as referring to that deep-down sense of who I am, that it is OK to be me, and that I can cope, somehow, with whatever comes along. I don't need to worry about getting my own needs met in the way I once did, though I still have to be responsible for taking care of myself. Knowing the difference saves me a lot of anxiety and enables me to step out of line if I want to. It also leaves me with spare energy to put into being Other-focused.

The other day I was at a concert. There was an empty seat beside me and then a youngish woman in the one beyond. Some time into the first item on the programme, I became aware that she was crying. I wondered what to do and then, at the end of the first movement, I leaned over and whispered: 'Would it help to talk?' She nodded so I said: 'Let's go out'. [Luckily we were near the end of a row]. We sat on the stairs and she told me why the seat beside her was empty. At the interval people negotiated their way around us.

After a while she felt better and we had a drink together. She decided to go home and gave me a hug at parting. The sense I now have of my own inside safety gave me the freedom not to have to worry about making a nuisance or a spectacle of myself: I could afford to be Other-focused: I was able to be GO-BI loving.

Moving from Self-focus to Other-focus

Most of our actions are partly Self-focused and partly Other-focused. We flick from one to the other as, second by second, we feel needy or safe in the situation in which we find ourselves. We don't often manage to look in one direction for very long. However the more we are able to accept that what is, is, to face our fears, to let go of wanting what we can't have, or to forgive those who have wronged us, the less we have clamouring for our attention inside. The 'Shall I? Shan't I?' debate is stilled. We become less concerned with keeping ourselves safe and more free to attend to other people. Periods of Other-focus lengthen and eventually we find we have a permanent orientation towards others so that it is natural to Go Out to and Bring In.

None of this can be achieved in a moment; it is a long, hard slog. Judith was hideously abused as a child, both physically and emotionally. In a most amazing way she has had a very successful career and is now involved in charity work. She works tirelessly, and very efficiently, for the good of others, and many people have benefited enormously from her care. Sometimes she believes she loves the people she works with, and that they love her. At other times she knows that she is deeply lonely and friendless, and only works to numb the pain and to try to fill the void inside. At these times Judith recognizes that what she does is a Self-focused attempt to make herself feel wanted and loved. Her Self-focus does not detract from the usefulness of her actions, but all her good works do not fill the aching void inside.

Her valuing of herself was so crushed as a child that she feels that she has not got a self worth giving - so she can't Go Out. Because she has not yet been able to overcome her fear of looking at those wounded parts of herself, she cannot let anyone else see them either - so she can't Bring-In. She can't GO-BI love. She is busy, lonely and friendless.

The only way I know for Judith to move from her defensive Self-focus to Other-focus is to allow herself to become aware of herself, which for her, means allowing herself to become aware of the horrors of her childhood. Not unnaturally, she doesn't want to do this. In moments of self-doubt, I think it is unreasonable for me even to suggest it to her. Then I remember all the other people who have fought their way down similar roads, over-coming all obstacles as they went. The people who have accepted what was, and still is in some cases; who have faced down their fears; who have let go of wanting what they can't have; who have forgiven those who have damaged them; have found themselves moving from Self-focus and loneliness to Other-focus and GO-BI loving. Then I believe it is worth it for Judith to keep working on all that keeps her from being the GO-BI loving person she wants to be.

Different Models of Loving

As I worked with the GO-BI loving idea I found that not only were there different kinds of loving; there were also different models of loving. There are some that are essentially the same as the Pass the Parcel Model; there are others that depend on getting our thoughts right – Thinking Models; and others that major on what we do - Behaviour Models.

Thinking Models

These models say that only love is real: everything else is the product of our imaginations, or illusion. This is certainly the case with fear, which is generated by our minds expecting something harmful to happen in the future; nothing is actually happening now. These models tell us that if we change our mind, which is always a very empowering thing to do, from negative, unreal thinking, to thinking loving thoughts our lives will run the way we want them to and we will be happy. This is broadly true but I don't much care for the way this model makes loving a method of achieving happiness. To me that sounds like making loving a means to an end, which is Self-focused.

The other problem with thinking models is that they assume we know what is meant by 'loving thoughts'. I didn't, which was why I asked my original question: 'What is love?' and came up with the answer: Going Out and Bringing In. I, personally, needed to know what love is before I could begin to think loving thoughts.

Behaviour Models

These mostly owe something to the famous thirteenth chapter of the Apostle Paul's First Letter to the Corinthians. His definition is a long list of qualities starting with: 'Love is patient, love is kind', and ending with; it 'always perseveres'.

The best thing about this model is that it is about actions, and therefore about choice. Paul says that love 'is not self-seeking' but the problem with a definition based on behaviours is that there is always a danger that our conduct will be Self-focused: we can be kind, and therefore appear loving, in order to get ourselves loved; we can persevere because we think that if we stick with it we will one day get our longed for pay-back of being loved. Love, as defined by Paul, is not proof against being inauthentic.

When we are being Self-focused our gaze is turned back on ourselves, so we can't make contact with the body, emotions, mind, and spirit of our intended beloved. GO-BI loving, on the other hand, is by definition, Other-focused: we have to look beyond ourselves, towards our intended beloved, if we are to Go Out, make the First Turn, and to Bring him or her In to ourselves.

Chapter 7

Ideas About Love

Misconceptions About Love

My thinking about different kinds of loving that either served our own purposes or were focused on other people brought me face to face with how widely the word 'love' is used. If the GO-BI loving idea was right and I was, by now, sure it was, then there were some contradictory ideas out there which needed looking at. Some of other people's ideas about what love is might, in themselves, prove to be obstacles to GO-BI loving.

We often talk of 'my love', as though it were a possession, something we own, that we can choose to give 'some of' to someone. The 'some of' carries implications of there being a finite amount of love at our disposal. We may not be aware that we think of love in terms of a 'thing', but how often, when someone we love forms a new relationship, have we felt afraid that we will somehow miss out, that something will be taken away from us in order to give it to the other person?

Many of us have been brought up in such a way that we have come to believe that love is conditional: that if we behave in a certain way or achieve a certain thing then we will be loved, but if not, not. Most of us have believed that love is, or at anyway ought to be, equal or at least mutual; that there cannot be such an activity as one-lover GO-BI loving.

Some poets and most popular song-writers think of love as a gooey feeling. It can be, but that particular state is more accurately described as 'being in love', which is different from loving. There is also a widely held connection between sex and love. They are not the same, though they can wonderfully co-exist and be an expression of each other.

There are problems with thinking of love in any of these ways if we are wanting to make those very specific movements of Going Out and Bringing In, which I have called GO-BI loving.

The Commodity Trap

The trouble with thinking about love as a thing is that a thing has size; there are outside edges to a thing, beyond which it cannot go. Love, thought of like this, becomes a commodity, like a bag of sugar. As soon as we start thinking this way we worry: 'Will I have enough to give – to make people love me?' or: 'Will there be enough to go round?' It's fine to think in terms of enough-ness when we are wondering how many sandwiches to cut for a picnic, but disastrous when we are considering loving.

Thinking of love as a thing, a commodity, takes us back into the Pass the Parcel Model: we must 'have some love' in order to pass it on as our love to someone else. Those of us who have very low self-esteem, who don't consider we are worth bothering with, who don't believe we have anything to give, are very often caught in the jaws of this trap.

There are two anxieties that show when we have got caught in the Commodity Trap. One is the: 'I won't have enough to give' and the other is the: 'Will there be enough to go round: for me to get some?' They are both to do with the concept of 'enough', which is about quantity.

I Won't Have Enough To Give

The debate going on between our body, emotions, mind and spirit, when we are in this mood, is derived from the Pass the Parcel Model of love. It goes something like this: 'I have nothing to give, [because I wasn't given anything], so I don't have enough to pass on'. GO-BI loving is the way out for those of us entangled is this sort of inside world argument. If we consider ourselves useless, worthless, a waste of space, boring, or ugly, to name a few of the ways we may feel about ourselves, then we are totally convinced that no one will want to love us or even be friends with us because we're not worth it; we don't have enough to give.

We have probably tried, in the past, to do the sort of things we feel might make us acceptable to other people, but if our efforts have been rejected, and if that rejection hurt – which it always does – we will be reluctant to try again. Clearly we don't have enough of what it takes. In that 'enough' we don't think of including that most precious of all gifts – our self. The giving of our self, however inadequate we may think we are, is a much more valuable gift, because it is more costly, than any 'amount of love' could ever be.

Enough to 'Make People...'

The other piece of tragic thinking in 'I won't have enough to give to make people want to love me' is the 'make people...' bit. There are two problems here. The first is 'make' and the second is 'people'. We can't make anyone do anything they don't want to, except by the use of force, and we can't even force them to feel, or to want, something they don't. However, many of us persist in the belief that if only we can 'get it right' – whatever 'it' might be – we will be loved. We continue to believe that loving relationships are possible and that if we try hard enough, we can make someone love us. We can't. It doesn't work like that.

The other problem is the word 'people', which in this context, is a generalization. We will almost certainly have experienced rejection by someone, but that someone was not people in general, i.e. everyone. This is incredibly hard to get into our heads, and when the penny finally does drop it is a wonderful moment. I have had counsellees say, with amazement, things like: 'I've been treating everyone as if they were my mother', or 'Not everyone is my Dad'.

When I first came to live in Winchester, I was well and truly stuck in the Commodity Trap. I assumed I had nothing to give, that there was nothing about me that was attractive, interesting, or in any way a desirable as an offering in friendship, let alone love. Part of the trouble was that I had no way of checking the truth of this belief, because I was too scared to Go Out and see what happened. When people approached me, I was sure that they did not really want me; that they were just being kind, so I refused the invitation they were giving, in order to spare them the boredom of my company. I thought I was being Other-focused but I wasn't. What they would have experienced was rejection. This is the major ill-effect of feeling rejected, we, in self defence, become rejecters.

Will There Be Enough To Go Round?

I first met the: 'Will there be enough to go round?' anxiety, many years ago in a dress-making client of mine. She already had a two year old son, Billy, whom she adored: 'He's such fun to be with' she once told me. She was now five months pregnant and asking me to design for her an evening dress for a very special 'do' at her husband's work.

The dressmaker and client relationship can become quite intimate and, during fittings of this dress, she confided to me that she was worried that she would not be able to love the new child as much as she loved Billy. At that stage in my life, I couldn't come up with anything more helpful to say than: 'I'm sure you will when the time comes'. This was, of course, true but I didn't understand how the extra loving comes about. I was simply hoping that it would.

My client felt she had given all of the loving she had for her children to Billy. She did not know, and more is the pity, neither did I, that her capacity to love would expand with the number of children to be loved. There was Billy's loving, the GO-BI loop created especially for him, and then there would the baby's new GO-BI loop, created especially for him or her. The two loops would be quite different. Giving herself to Billy and Bringing him In to herself would be totally different from giving herself to, and Bringing In the new baby when he or she was born. Her two GO- BI loving loops would be distinctive, unique, special, for each of them. And the children would experience that specialness even though they would now have to share her time and attention. When we understand love as Going Out and Bringing In, rather than something we have, it is perfectly obvious that, for Billy's Mum, when the new baby arrives, all she will have to do is create a new GO-BI loving loop. We can always do more GO-BI loving; we don't always have more of a thing to hand out.

It is also perfectly possible to make another GO-BI loop around a new friend without taking any loving from an old friend, or even a committed partner. Certain things, like sexual intercourse and living together, are best kept as special, and precious, to committed partnerships but I do not believe that this precludes creating deep, but different, GO-BI lovings outside these particular committed, contracted, our-relationships. Not to be able to do this brings huge impoverishment to body, emotions, mind and spirit, for many who know they have the spare capacity to form more than one loop of GO-BI loving.

Will I Get My Share?

Thinking of love as a thing with finite dimensions raises another question: 'Will I get my share?' This is very similar to: 'Will there be enough to go round?' in that they are both rooted in thing-thinking and measurement. The difference is that 'Will I get my share?' is about fair distribution. The love cake may be big enough for everyone, but we are worried about the size of our slice: will it be as big as we think it should be, or that someone else has. And will it have as many cherries?

The thing called love is also sometimes measured in quality time spent together. A new father can feel he is not getting his fair share of his wife's love because so much of her time is now taken up with the baby. The GO-BI loving can remain the same but its expression will have to change with the changed circumstances.

Gifts can be another way of measuring love, or they can even be mistaken for love itself. I once worked with Will. When he was a child his father used to make long business trips and then come back bearing gifts. Will felt these showed how much his Dad loved him. Then one time Will wanted to show his Dad an aeroplane he had made. Instead of being interested Dad told him to go away and play with his present. It was painful for Will to recall this incident and to have to accept that the presents were a substitute for love; a way of keeping him quiet while Dad caught up with his Mum.

Of course, gifts can be given as tokens or symbols of loving but that is different. The GO-BI loving is there already, the gift is simply an outward and visible sign of it. For Will the gifts were a substitute for, not an expression of, love.

Thinking of Love As a 'Gooey Feeling'

Many people think that 'love' is that wobbly-kneed, heart-stopping, waiting for the phone or text, gooey feeling which is so wonderful and so all consuming. This, to my mind, is being in-love, which is not at all the same as GO-BI loving. Being in-love is a heady mixture of hormones and a deep need to find, in our beloved, some part of ourselves that seems to be missing. In the closeness of our embraces; in the depth of our kissing; we are straining to find that place where we are no longer alone. 'In-love-ness' is the glorious mechanism which, for some people, ensures the continuation of the species.

These wonderful feelings are, to a large extent, Self-focused. They are what we want to get for ourselves from our lover, and from being in-love. The state is not meant to last. It is the job of in-love-ness to bring us together; it is the job of GO-BI loving to keep us together. I read recently in *Small Boat, Big Sea* by Peter Owen Jones that: 'Marriage is the cauldron of love, the place where we actually learn to love once we have recovered from falling in love'.

This was where Ruth and Iain were when they came to see me; painfully stewing in the cauldron of love. They had done the in-love bit. They had got through their first big row; kissed and made up. But it was not the same. The gloss had gone from their relationship and they couldn't see what to do about it.

Because of where they were in their individual growing, they were both still looking at what was happening from their own point of view: they were being Self-focused. In-love-ness can't cope when the going gets tough. They needed something more robust. They needed to start GO-BI loving.

The first thing was to learn how to forgive each other for not being the wonderful people that their in-love-ness had suggested they were. They had discovered that they were not going to find all their needs met in each other. [Romantic fiction has a lot to answer for.] More importantly, they each also needed to learn to forgive themselves for the disappointment they felt in their marriage. This is a terrible feeling. It is compounded of guilt and sadness, and can drive a wedge between two people. Lastly they needed to learn to dare to give themselves with all their fears, faults and weaknesses and to be generous enough to receive each other's fears, faults and weaknesses. They needed to practice GO-BI loving.

Together we worked on each of them becoming more aware of themselves as a whole person with a body, emotions, a mind and a spirit. This helped them to become more aware of each other in the same way. They began to move from Self-focus – this is all about me, to Other-focus - seeing more of the fullness of each other.

Their in-love-ness, which was what brought them together in the first place, will grow, through years of bearing each other's frailties and forgiving each other, into a deep, mature, Mutual GO-BI loving. [See the bottom doodle on the cover.] I hope their loving will not lose any of its first freshness and rapture, but I know there is now also a deep, trusting, giving, and receiving of each other. They are set for a long, committed, learning to love.

I hear from them occasionally. Their GO-BI loving is still growing, and has sprouted another GO-BI-loop to go round a baby girl.

Thinking Love Has To Be Mutual

Need For a Guarantee

Another false idea about love is that it has to be mutual: most of us don't want to contemplate a loving that is not two-way. One reason for this is that we feel it is safer to love if we think we are being loved. It is a sort of guarantee that we will not be rejected if we dare to Go Out and to Bring In. This is particularly important if, in the past, we have experienced our approach being turned down, ridiculed or even ignored. The best way to keep ourselves safe - we think - is to hang back until our intended beloved makes a move in our direction. We wait, and we wait until we believe that we have a guarantee that our loving will be returned. There are people who spend their whole lives in loneliness, playing this waiting game.

When I was a young adult I had a 'One in Three Rule' of only accepting every third invitation from the same young man. This was an attempt to provide myself with a cast iron guarantee that he really, really must want to see me, making it safe for me to Go-Out to him and to Bring him In. Any loving, if we ever got that far, would be mutual. However, not surprisingly, few of them did want to see me that much. I found I had provided myself with a neat little self-fulfilling prophesy; 'I was right wasn't I? He doesn't want to know me, does he?', and a perfect excuse for not venturing out of my safety zone - my lonely zone - again. I went on waiting for my guarantee.

Fairness

A further reason for thinking loving should be mutual has to do with fairness: 'Why should I love her when she doesn't love me?' This question also has an element of need for a guarantee of reciprocity in it, but it is mostly about: 'What's in it for me?', the Self-focused, thing-thinking, notion of getting some sort of return on our investment.

Fairness is also involved where one party fails to deliver a promised mutual loving. The question then is: 'Why should I give more than she is giving?' This may be a childish response but, if thinking of love as a commodity is the only way we know, when we are in a relationship which is not giving us the return we want, our Self-focused way of coping is bound to be: 'I'm not getting what I was promised. It's not fair. I'm not going to play anymore.' We don't know, because we haven't heard or we haven't thought about it, that being Other-focused in one-lover GO-BI loving does bring its own amazing rewards.

Thinking That Love Is Conditional

Conditional love is a contradiction in terms, because for love to be love at all it must be free: without conditions. Love always has the two elements of accepting the beloved as they are, and of being a free gift. We love each other in spite of our weaknesses and our irritating little habits. We give our loving because we choose to, and for no other reason. There are, however, kinds of 'love' which are Self-focused and that do demand certain conditions.

Performance-linked Love

The other day I heard a mother say: 'Oh, you stupid girl. See what a mess you've made', when Ellie, her small daughter, spilled her drink. With these words the mother told Ellie that she was not acceptable, not lovable, when she was performing in the 'wrong' way.

Performance-linked loving can also be applied to behaviour that is acceptable. I worked with Jim, whose father was immensely proud of him but could only express himself negatively. Jim remembered getting 100% in a maths test and his Dad saying: 'Only 100%. Dear, oh dear, whatever next?' Jim didn't see the joke and despaired of ever being good enough to be loved by his Dad. The sad thing was that I am sure his Dad thought he was being loving but he had a skewed idea of what loving really is.

Trying to do the right thing by someone else's standards in order to be loved is, of course, Self-focused behaviour. It is trying to manipulate someone into loving us by doing what they want. If that is the only way we know how to meet our desperate need to be loved, we will do it with all our might and ingenuity.

Most of my life I have believed I was wrong to the very core of my being. I consequently tried to move heaven and earth to get something, anything, right. I drove myself mercilessly and exhausted myself trying to please. All to no avail. I felt I could not 'get it right' in my outside world because I believed I was totally and irremediably wrong in my inside world. I was linking any possible GO-BI loving of myself to my performance and finding myself wanting.

Earned Love

That love can be earned is another fallacy. 'If I do what you want, you will give me my wages of love.' If we do the most we can and still don't get paid with the love we long for, we probably feel angry. We may also feel rejected: our best was not good enough to be rewarded with love. This can lead to turning in on ourselves, despair and, eventually, to giving up on life. It is simply too much effort to go on trying.

Love and Roles

There is a mistaken idea that love happens automatically when people are in particular roles. 'My parents [should] love me'. 'I [ought] to love my wife'. These 'shoulds' and 'oughts' set up expectations that love is part of the role: that it comes with the territory. I have to tell you: it doesn't.

Loving comes because one person chooses to give themselves in loving to another, whether that person is their child, their spouse, or their friend: simply because they want to. There is no assumption, no 'ought' or 'should' about it. Love is the free gift of the lover.

We are being Self-focused when we put expectations on roles because they are a subtle way of exerting pressure to make people be the way we want them to be. Of course it is highly desirable that parents love their children, that husbands and wives love each other, that members of communities have loving relationships, but the loving does not come with the roles, it comes because each individual is choosing to love.

Thinking of Love As 'Sex'

The final mistaken belief about love that I want to look at is that it is sex. The word sex is used to convey many different meanings. For the present purposes, I shall be using 'sex' in the colloquial sense of 'having sex': sexual intercourse. It is in this meaning that sex is sometimes equated with love. I heard it beautifully put by an ex-prostitute on the radio the other day. She said simply: 'Having sex is not making love'. She was right.

The distinction she was drawing was between sex that is simply intended as physical pleasure, and sex that is part of creating a mutual loving: in a very real sense 'making love'. Sex is Self- focused when it is primarily intended for the individual's pleasure, even if both parties happen to be enjoying it.

The: 'Was it alright?' following Self-focused sex, is usually more about wanting to be told that the performance was good, than wanting to know how it felt for the partner. The 'chemistry' may have been right, but their awareness of each other did not extend beyond their bodies having the exhilarating capacity for setting off each other's hormones. If this is their idea of the height of sexual experience it is sad. They are missing out on the ecstasy of loving with the whole of themselves: body, of course, but emotions, mind and spirit as well, fusing into one GO-BI loving.

Sex that is part of the expression of Mutual GO-BI loving is Other-focused. It is one of the many ways of Going Out from ourselves and Bringing In our beloved. When lovers - that is those who are already loving each other - engage in sexual inter-course, it has all the joy of expressing their mutual self giving, their Going Out and Bringing In, with the added delight of physical union.

Love Without Sex

The phrase 'making love', as a euphemism for sexual inter-course, is unhelpful when it leads a couple to thinking: 'If we are not having sex, we are not loving each other'. The confusion arises because the partners have forgotten, or never known, that sex is only one of ways of expressing loving. It can be very important to understand this if a couple want to love each other but can't, for some reason, have sexual intercourse.

Paul had an illness which made intercourse with his wife, Sally, impossible for him. They both worried that they were not loving or being loved properly, because they couldn't 'make love'. As we talked about the problem they realized that what they were concerned about was how to express their Mutual GO-BI loving with their bodies. Once they understood what they were wanting to do, their imaginations were freed to find all sorts of other physical ways of communicating their loving. They have found that 'sex' is not an absolute requirement for a deep and full Mutual GO-BI loving between two people.

Sex Without Love

The flip side of thinking: 'We can't be loving if we are not having sex' is: 'If we are having sex, we must be loving'. Regarding sex and love as more or less the same thing can lead to abuse of a partner. I have worked with a woman whose husband was sexually violent with her, satisfying his own needs while disregarding her personhood. She hated, and was physically hurt by, the things he did, but, on the rare occasions that she mustered the courage to complain, he simply said: 'This is how I love my wife'. For him sex and love meant the same thing, so that any abusive sexual action went by the name of love, and was, therefore, perfectly justified.

Sex without love can range from the quick shag in the stationery room at the office party when both partners are a bit the worse for wear and neither remember much about it the next morning, to the rape that leaves a man or a woman scarred for life.

Love That Overcomes

However, I do know one deeply moving story where the husband was practicing sex without love but his wife was managing to one-lover GO-BI love him. I had long known that Amy struggled with her sexual relationship with her husband. His idea of sexual intercourse was of the 'Wham, bam', and if she was lucky, 'Thank you, Mam,' variety. She longed for something deeper; the mutual loving of which she knew herself capable. It never happened. Amy is as well versed in the principles of GO-BI loving as I am, so one night, when her husband wanted to have 'sex', she thought to herself: 'I can GO-BI love him; I can give myself to him and bring him in, even if he is not doing the same to me'. She told me she held him really tight and willed herself to Go- Out to him and to Bring him In, with the whole of herself. Something happened. She could not explain what exactly, but she knew that she experienced something wonderful that she had never felt before. 'And', she said, 'I think he felt something too'. This was one-lover GO-BI loving of an awesomely high order. Incredibly, these things do happen.

A note of realism: everything was not transformed from that

moment on; Amy and her husband did not live happily ever after. There were still bad times when she felt used and abused. But she knew that when she had the strength, and it took a lot of strength, something magnificent was possible.

The Problem With These Ideas About Love

Wrong ideas about what loving is constitute obstacles to GO-BI loving. It is hard to do anything if we don't have a very clear idea of what it is that we are trying to do. It is hard to Go Out or to Bring In if there are bits of us saying: 'Don't do that. You'll get hurt'. The sensible thing to do in that case is to stay put; but then we stay lonely, unloving and unloved. We need to look at the obstacles to GO-BI loving; the fears, the holdings on to people or ideas, the lack of self-awareness or the being unreal about ourselves or our intended beloved, all of which can get in the way of our Going Out and Bringing In.

Chapter 8

Obstacles to GO-BI Loving

Self-focus and Fear

When we decide not to make a move to start GO-BI loving, it is always because our body, emotions, mind and spirit are being Self-focused: they are looking inwards to meet their own needs rather than being able to look out, and to Go Out, towards the person we want to love. Self-focus makes us hold on to people or things that make us feel safe. Self-focus very often gets in the way of being aware of ourselves because we are so concerned with one particular aspect of ourselves that we fail to get the big picture. Self-focus can also lead us to create an unreal picture of ourselves or someone else; how we want to be, or how we want them to be rather than how we, or they, actually are. All these occasions for Self-focus have their roots in fear. They are about trying to keep ourselves safe because we are afraid. To GO-BI love is always a risky enterprise, so any impulse to stay in our safety zone rather than reaching out, is going to be a serious obstacle to GO-BI loving.

Fear is the strongest negative argument that one or another of our body, emotions, mind and spirit can throw into the 'Shall I? Shan't I?' debate. It is sometimes very obvious that we are afraid, at other times our fear is hidden under another emotion. We may feel sad but under the sadness is a fear that we will never find again something we have lost. Fear is what we feel when we expect we are going to be hurt, physically or emotionally, so it is a significant deterrent to Going Out and Bringing In. I am not going to reach out again, and risk losing, because losing hurts too much. Unless we can overcome, get round, over, or through, this obstacle of fear we will not be able to Go Out or to Bring In when that is really what we want to do. We will not be able to GO-BI love, so we will not be able to feel loved.

How Do We Get To Be Afraid?

There seem to be two factors involved in getting to be afraid. One is learning through experience, the other is that, either through repetition of an experience or the deep significance of it, we form an expectation that it will happen again.

If we experience something – going to the park and having fun or being pushed into the swimming pool before we could swim – we then know what it is like for those things to happen. We file that information in our memory. When we are approaching a similar situation again we know, from experience, whether to go for it or to do our best to avoid it.

It was fun in the park so we expect it to be fun again and look forward to another visit: it was scary being thrown into the pool so we don't want to go swimming again. If it was really terrifying and we thought we were going to drown, then that one incident will be enough to put us off swimming for life. The worse the past experience, the fewer repeats it takes for us to expect it to be bad in future.

Fear works like this: past experience feeds into our present thinking and forms an expectation which we project onto the future. So through experience of something bad and the expectation that it will happen again, we experience fear in the now. The expected fear-inducing thing is still in the future, but the fear is felt now. This can make understanding what is making us afraid quite tricky. We usually have to dig around in the past to find what is feeding into our present thinking and making us expect the worst in the future.

If my past experience, when I reached out to someone, was to be rejected then I will expect to be rejected again so my present behaviour will probably be to keep myself to myself. I feel this even if it is my intended beloved I want to reach out to, and the future I long for is only a smile away. Fear will be preventing me from Going Out or Bringing In.

Feeling Threatened

We call expecting something bad to happen feeling threatened. Feeling threatened makes us behave in one of three ways: fight, flight or freeze. They all have an element of keeping ourselves at a safe distance from whatever it is that is threatening us. For this reason I call all feelings with fear at their roots 'self-distancing' emotions.

Fight might seem like a get-in-close response: we have to be near someone to hit them, the most basic form of fighting, but we only want to hit them in order to get rid of them. It is getting close in order to drive away. We can, of course, use more long-distance weapons like words, but the effect is the same: we are trying to put a distance between ourselves and whoever, or whatever, is threatening us.

Flight is very obviously about putting space between ourselves and the object of our fear. We can do this physically, by lurking in the kitchen rather than joining the party, or we can do it emotionally by withdrawing into ourselves rather than reaching out to create a relationship or to start GO-BI loving.

When we are so afraid that we can't even make either of these responses, we freeze. Our minds and/or our bodies simply shut down. We may not be able to move our body as in those 'The Bogey Man is coming to get you' games which are such fun for some people and so panic-inducing for others. Alternatively, our mind may 'go blank' like when we are asked to work out a sum and there is only white cloud in our head. In shutting down we are denying the existence of whatever it is that we fear.

Because of these ways in which we respond to feeling afraid, all of which are distancing or cutting-off, fear becomes a huge obstacle to GO-BI loving, which is all about the closeness and intimacy of daring to give ourselves and to have our intended beloved as part of our own being. We simply cannot do this if we are significantly afraid.

However, the broken line in the GO-BI loving doodle shows us that we can still Go Out with the bits of ourselves that are not afraid, and we can Bring In the bits of our intended beloved that we are not too scared to have as part of ourselves. We can always start GO-BI loving, once we have decided to. We can fill in some of the gaps in our line as we learn to face down our fears, making us able to GO-BI love more fully.

Self-distancing Emotions

Fear gets everywhere. Sometimes it is very obvious, like fear of big dogs or walking under ladders. We know about it and we just don't go there. We may not be so aware of fear when it is hidden under another emotion. Blame has fear of being wrong at its root; worry is fear of not knowing what is going to happen next. I call emotions which are rooted in fear 'self-distancing' because, in one way or another, they all drive us to fighting, fleeing, or freezing, all of which make us essentially unavailable for Going Out or Bringing In. The most significant self-distancing emotions are Rejection, Shame, Guilt, Distrust, and Anger.

The problem with these big self-distancing emotions is that they are usually generalized, by which I mean that we think: 'I am afraid of rejection', rather than: 'I was hurt that time when Janet didn't ask me to go on holiday with her'. For safety's sake we apply the learning from a specific experience to similar events in general. This makes these self-distancing emotions very difficult to get away from. Any similar event can trigger them, and then we are flipped into one of the fear responses which are going in the opposite direction to GO-BI loving. How far or how fast we retreat from Going Out and Bringing In depends on where we are on the sliding scale of any self-distancing emotion which runs from 'mildly discomforting' to 'so awful that we feel life is not worth living'.

Rejection

Rejection is one of the easiest to recognize as having fear at its root. Most of us know it is terrible to feel unwanted, abandoned or left on our own. We fear that bottom-dropping-out-of-our-world feeling and do anything we can to avoid it. When our approach has been repulsed or ignored once or twice we may keep trying but if it goes on happening we think: 'Blow this for a game of soldiers. I'm not doing that again. It hurts too much. And I'm going to make sure you don't come near me, for the same reason'. The tragedy is that, having been rejected; we start playing 'tit for tat' and become rejecters. It is the only way we have found for keeping ourselves safe. This pattern can set in very early in childhood.

I remember a time when I must have been three or four and Mum was ill in bed. I took her some pretend tea in a toy bucket. There was a drop of muddy water in the bottom which spilled on the bed. I can see the black blob spreading on the whiteness of the sheet even now. Mum, not unnaturally, was cross, but I felt she was rejecting me in rejecting my effort to reach out to her. In the past I have often not reached out to other people. I have rejected them because I have been afraid that they would be cross and reject me. I have kept my distance – and my isolation.

Fear of rejection can go beyond the isolation brought about by the 'tit for tat' response. It can affect our sense of security in being who we are, or even that we are, which we get from being loved and accepted. If a baby or a small child is not loved; is rejected by his or her chief carer, the worst case scenario could be abandonment leading to death. This may sound a bit extreme, but I believe that, very deep down, we do have some apprehension of ceasing to exist if we are radically rejected. This accounts for our agonizing fear of rejection.

Looked at from the receiving end, it is always worth remembering that, when someone rejects us, it is probably because they are afraid of being rejected. Knowing this does not lessen our pain but it may help us not to get caught in the 'I'll reject you because you rejected me' trap.

Shame

This is a seriously self-distancing emotion because it is about wanting to keep ourselves hidden. We can't Go Out if we are afraid to be seen. We can't Bring In, even in our inside world, if we are afraid to have anyone knowing us.

When we are told that we are not up to the mark in some way we feel shame that another person has exposed a weakness that we were trying to keep hidden. If this happens in front of a crowd, like a class full of children or a group of friends, then it is even worse: they all now know our secret; we want the floor to open up and swallow us. This is the outside aspect of shame.

Shame also has an inside aspect: we can feel ashamed in front of ourselves, which is why I put it among the most significant self-distancing emotions. We have that same feeling of wanting not to be there when we discover something that we don't like about ourselves.

I woke up one morning with the shocking realization that I had fallen in love with a counsellee. I had only been dimly aware that I took particular care with how I dressed on the day that he came, and that I always had flowers in my counselling room because he had once admired them. I felt deeply ashamed to find that I was the sort of person who could do such a profoundly unprofessional thing. I plunged into a crisis of confidence because, underneath my shame, there was the permanent fear that I was not good enough: that I would never be good enough; that there was an absolute impossibility of me ever getting anything right. It was a bad time and I was so engrossed in it that I could not have Gone Out to anyone, nor Brought them In, even if I had known about GO-BI loving, which I didn't at the time. I felt I needed to distance myself from everyone in case they found out what I had found out about myself.

Guilt

Guilt is very similar to shame before ourselves. We feel guilty when we accuse ourselves of some particular transgression; when we have hurt or upset someone; have transgressed our own code of behaviour; or have broken one of society's laws that we believe to be a just one. Other people or a court of law may accuse us, and find us guilty, when we have broken one of their rules. If it is one we don't subscribe to we probably won't feel guilty about what we have done. Conscientious objectors are a prime example of this.

The fear behind guilt is of finding ourselves despicable, rotten to the core, and therefore unworthy to associate with other people: we make ourselves outcasts. In our inside world we are ringing a bell and crying: 'Unclean! Unclean!', which is not a position from which it is possible to Go Out or to Bring In, in GO-BI loving of other people or ourselves.

Distrust

If we have come to expect that our needs will not be met, that we will not be loved, that we will be let down or betrayed, we will grow up deficient in trust of ourselves and everyone else. We will expect the worst. Meister Eckhart, who was writing in the thirteenth century, said: 'Love cannot distrust, it trustfully awaits [expects] only good'. Put the other way round: 'We cannot love, if we await [or expect] only bad'. It is very hard to Go-Out if we are expecting only bad; to be hurt or taken advantage of. It is equally hard to Bring In if we are expecting to be let down or ignored. The fact that this is an expectation, not a known fact about the future, makes no difference at all to the way we feel because the fear is in the space between the now and the future expectation. It tells us: 'You can't assume anyone is going to help you or to love you', and so we react with one of the responses to fear which are such an obstacle to GO-BI loving.

Anger

When we know that we feel rejected, ashamed, guilty or distrustful, we may also know that it did not have to be this way. We know that there is something that we should have now, or should have had in the past, that is missing, and that something is love. We search for it and if we don't find it we get frustrated. If we keep trying and keep being thwarted our frustration eventually explodes as anger and we don't want to be near whoever we believe is causing our distress.

Stuart, the teenage son of a friend of mine, had a terrible screaming match with his father the other day, stormed out of the house and was missing for 36 hours. The trigger was not being allowed to go out until he had finished his college project. What erupted was an accumulation of similar frustrations which turned into anger against his Dad. The underlying fear for Stuart was that, by preventing him doing what he wanted, his Dad was saying that he did not love his son.

Other Self-distancing Emotions

Loss is often a self-distancing emotion. It may, as Tennyson said, be 'better to have loved and lost than never to have loved at all', but the losing can still be excruciatingly painful. Mark's relationship had just broken up. He was distraught and vowed he would never get close to another girl. The thought that the same thing might happen again made him afraid to Go Out to, or to Bring In anyone else. He came to me because he was lonely. That's the cost of keeping ourselves at a safe distance.

Envy and Jealousy are usually self-distancing emotions. They both have fear underlying them; fear of not having something we think that, by rights, we should – envy – or fear that what we have will be taken away from us and given to another – jealousy. Lynda was estranged from her family and when she first met Julie they seemed to get on. However after a while Lynda began to struggle because she could not bear to see Julie with her Mum and Dad and two brothers. They were the family she felt she should have had and, deep down, she hated Julie for having them instead of her. Her envy proved an obstacle to her GO-BI loving her friend.

The Grip Of Fear

When we are in the grip of fear, our body, emotions, mind and spirit will say: 'This is too painful. We can't cope' and we become emotionally unavailable for any sort of Going Out or Bringing In. Sometimes they will even say: 'We're getting out of here'. Then we dissociate and have that out-of-body sensation that feels as though we are looking at ourselves from a corner of the ceiling. Those who have suffered extreme trauma will recognize this experience. When we are in that state we are beyond even Self-focus; we cannot connect with ourselves, let alone anybody else, so GO-BI loving is completely out of the question.

Being caught in any of these self-distancing emotions will stop us GO-BI loving. We will protect ourselves from hurt by keeping at a safe distance. This may satisfy a part of us, but there may be other parts which sincerely want to love. The great 'Shall I? Shan't I?' debate then starts up again in our body, emotions, mind and spirit: 'What shall we do?' 'Keep safe and be lonely or take a risk and Go Out and Bring In?' There are times when it doesn't seem much of a choice; we don't want to be alone and we don't want to risk being close. There is fear whichever way we look.

Holding On

Another significant obstacle to GO-BI loving is holding on. We can hold on to a person, a dream or a belief about ourselves. If we allow it to be the only thing we want we can never look at anything else. We can never Go Out and create a new loop of GO-BI loving.

This is what happened to Mandy. Her father had been absent, emotionally and physically, for most of her childhood and she found that now she had a distant relationship with him. She longed to have a father who was there for her, and did things with her, who she could talk to. This dream Dad was getting in the way of her being close to her real Dad. 'Real Dad' simply did not measure up to 'Dream Dad'. She needed to stop holding on to the dream before she could think of Going Out and Bringing In the reality. There is a way of dealing with this sort of situation which I write about later.

Lack of Self-Awareness

Without being aware of ourselves we won't be listening to what is going on between our body, emotions, mind and spirit. We won't be able to identify what is happening in the 'Shall I? Shan't I?' debate. We won't know whether we think it is safe to Go Out and to Bring In or not.

I have been working with James who hated himself, but he did not know why. All he could say to begin with was: 'I'm all wrong'. This was obviously a huge obstacle to his Going Out or Bringing In. How could he give himself and bring another deep into himself if he was all wrong inside?

By doing various exercises that helped him to hear what his body, emotions, mind and spirit were saying we discovered that, deep down, he had always wanted to be a girl. He felt he would have been loved by his Mum and got to spend more time with her, if he had been a girl. This awareness helped him to see that it was his Mum's love that he wanted; he didn't really want to be a girl. He was able to accept himself as the man he was which gave him a self to Go Out with and, in the fullness of time, he was able to Bring In a very special girl.

Being unaware of what is going on inside ourselves leads us, in an odd way, to being Self-focused. This is because we are only hearing part of the story: we know that we want to feel loved and we try our hardest to meet our own need. However, without being aware of the painful bit about why we feel unloved we are stuck, and can't make the move from wanting to be loved to loving.

When we have 'no go' areas inside ourselves, or don't understand what is going on in the 'Shall I? Shan't I?' debate, we don't feel safe in being who we are. Lack of self-awareness leads to a diminished sense of identity and security, which, in turn, lead to not being able to trust: all serious obstacles to Going Out and Bringing In.

Being Unreal

Being unreal is not quite the same as lack of self-awareness. Instead of simply not noticing ourselves, we, unconsciously perhaps, set out to create a different, more acceptable self because we are afraid that our real self is not good enough or that we can't cope with being the way we are. We can also be unreal by creating different, more acceptable, intended beloveds. If we are Going Out with an unreal self or are trying to Bring In an unreal intended beloved, there is bound to be something unreal about our GO-BI loving.

Being real about ourselves means accepting that this is the way we are. This is the real me. I don't particularly like certain bits of me, but they are me and I can't get away from the fact. Being real about other people also means accepting them as they are.

I have a friend, Jackie, whose life is fairly complicated and she does not always manage it quite as well as she might. One Monday she arrived for coffee at 10.30. I was not expecting her until the following day. She was absolutely adamant that the mistake was mine. I had a meeting at 11.00 on the Monday which had been in my diary for several weeks so I was sure I would not have asked her to coffee at 10.30. She would have none of it. 'I wrote it down for to-day and I don't make mistakes. You must have got it wrong'. She could not accept as real that part of her that was capable of putting something down on the wrong day in her diary – like the rest of us do now and again. Denying the I-can-make-mistakes part of herself made her blame me – somebody had to be wrong - and blame is a self-distancing emotion and, therefore, an obstacle to GO-BI loving.

The Power of Decisions

With so many obstacles to GO-BI loving it is a wonder that we ever manage to Go Out or Bring In at all. That we do is due to the decisions we make. If we choose to become aware of the obstacles to our GO-BI loving and choose to overcome them, then that is what we will do. We will come to accept what is and let go of the unrealities that we have been clinging on to. We will face down our fears and forgive ourselves and other people for the things that are making us guilty or angry. And the good news is that there are tools which we can use to help us make these life transforming changes in the way we think and feel. And the further good news is that we don't have to wait until we have done it all before we can do some loving. Each time we make a change we fill in one of the gaps in our broken line of Going Out and Bringing In, and we find we are living more fully and GO-BI loving more deeply.

Part 2

Tools for Overcoming Obstacles to GO-BI Loving

The Tool Kit

If fear, with its consequent self-distancing emotions, holding on, lack of self-awareness, and not being real are the broad categories of obstacles to GO-BI loving, is there anything we can do about them? The answer is: 'Yes'. There are tools that we can use to help us overcome them all, but first we have to be sufficiently self-aware to recognize that we are up against an obstacle to GO-BI loving.

When we are stuck in not being real Accepting is the tool to use. When we accept we are choosing to leave our perceived 'safety' of Cloud Cuckoo Land and to step into the Real World.

When we hold ideas about ourselves or other people that make us isolate ourselves, or when we are in the grip of self-distancing emotions like anger; or are hanging on to someone in the present or the past, or are so caught in a dream that we can't live in reality, we need to be able to detach ourselves. The tool for this is Letting go. We can also be fiercely attached to the debts we are owed – 'And you didn't remember our anniversary' [the first one; 20 years ago.] To release ourselves from hauling this sort of burden of grievance around for years, we can use another form of letting go: Forgiving.

We may simply be afraid or fear may lie at the root of another emotion. Either way we can use the tool of Facing Down Fear to set ourselves free. All of us suffer, at some time or another, from one or more of the self-distancing emotions that have fear at their root. They are perfectly natural but they are an obstacle to GO-BI loving, especially if we get bogged down in them. We often need to use Accepting to acknowledge that we have a problem, in the first place, before we can use the appropriate tool to overcome it. I am being unreal if I say: 'I don't really like my boss, but it doesn't matter. I get along OK', when the truth is that I am afraid of her. I will first have to accept that fact that I am afraid before I can do anything to overcome my fear.

Chapter 9

Accepting

What Accepting Is

Accepting is empowering because it is an act of will. It is choosing to move from: 'I don't want it to be so' to: 'That is the way it is. And I don't need it to be any different, in order to get on with my life'. Not accepting becomes an obstacle to GO-BI loving when what we 'don't want to be so' is something connected with our intended beloved. In order to be able to Go Out and Bring In we need to get ourselves to the place from which we can say: 'I don't need my intended beloved to have done other than she did'. 'I don't need him to be other than he is'. What we are accepting is the 'is-ness' of the person or their actions. Accepting is being able to say: 'That is the way it is', which gives us the freedom then to add: 'Now what, if anything, shall I do about it?'

By accepting we are *not* saying: 'Because it is, it is OK that it is'. The way people are, the things they do, can be deeply wrong but that does not, alas, prevent them from being facts. To accept is not to make a value judgment. It is not saying it is right or wrong, good or bad. It is simply saying: 'It is'.

No Getting Away from the Fact

Acknowledging that someone we love has a drink or drugs problem; admitting the fact that our partner doesn't like the films and shows that we do; taking a long, hard look at the fact that the friend we trusted has let us down, recognizing that we can't do as much as we used to, can all be very painful. There is a part of us that would rather turn a blind eye and try to carry on as usual.

If we really could remain unaware we probably would be able

to carry on as usual. The trouble is that we can't. We may pretend not to see, or not to mind, but the fact is that we do. As long as we live in unreality we will feel a niggling worry, resentment, or hurt and that will get in the way of our Going Out and our Bringing In.

We can deny facts in little ways as well as big ones; we can deny positive facts as well as negative ones; we can deny facts about ourselves or other people. A while ago I found myself getting very angry with a friend, Diana, who is always putting herself down. Wondering why her behaviour got to me so badly a voice inside me asked: 'Could it be anything to do with not liking in other people what you don't like in yourself?'

'Could be' another part of me replied.

I have had the greatest difficulty in accepting the fact that I am good at anything and, though I don't put myself down in the obvious way Diana does, I still sometimes feel inferior to the company in which I find myself. Not accepting the fact that I am good at some things has led me to brush aside compliments which must have been hurtful, or annoying, to whoever was saying something kind. I have had to accept that I am good at some things in order to GO-BI love myself more fully which, in turn, has enabled me to Bring In other people - and their compliments - and Diana with her tendency to put herself down.

Condoning

Accepting can also be used to resolve much bigger problems than getting niggled with a friend. I worked with Bill. He came to me because his daughter had said that he ought to: she was worried about her parents. Bill's wife, Isobel, was 'fond of her tipple'. While Bill was still working he noticed she sometimes seemed a little vague or clumsy when he got home in the evenings but he thought nothing of it. They always had a drink before their meal and, at weekends, wine with it. She usually had a glass or two more than he did. As that was what she liked he didn't see there was any harm in it. Then, the previous year, going to a coffee morning, she had crashed her car. She was over the limit and lost her licence. That had shaken them both at the time, but by then he had retired so he could drive her around: he quite liked having something to do.

As he had come to me to please his daughter, I asked him what he would like counselling to do for him. He obviously had not thought about it so he hesitated before it all came out in a rush.

'I love my wife very much. I don't know what I would do without her. I earned the money but she has always run our lives. Deep down I know that she is drinking too much – dangerously – but she would be so hurt if I said anything. I can't do it'.

Poor Bill. He had been condoning Isobel's drinking for years. He hoped that if he ignored it, somehow it would go away. He thought he was loving her but in fact, by condoning her excessive drinking, he was denying who she really was, a woman with a problem, and he was being Self-focused in saving himself the pain of upsetting her. He was not Going Out to her – his fear of hurting her kept him back – nor was he Bringing In the whole of her - drink problem included, because he did not want it to be so. Bill needed the tool of accepting to bring him to the place where he could say: 'Isobel has a drink problem. That is what is'. Then he would be able to Bring her In even more deeply than he did already.

Having decided to talk Bill was able to tell me about the time when she had been sick on the stairs, and the time when she talked non-sense at a dinner party, and the time when she cut her hand so badly trying to fillet a fish that he had to take her to casualty: in the snow. He had had a very tough time trying to pretend Isobel didn't have a problem.

I asked him what had been the worst bit: what was hardest to accept. He said: 'Not so much the things she did: it was more the way she looked.'

'How was that?'

'Sort of damp round the mouth, and bloated – she put on a lot of weight. She was all bleary; not focused. And she smelt.' He added, almost inaudibly: 'She's revolting'. There it was; out.

I had had an idea so I asked him if he had ever held her when she was like that.

'No. I can't. I usually leave the room.'

This was the opening I had been looking for. I had recently read the account of St. Francis of Assisi embracing the leper which had seemed to me a radical form of accepting that enabled him to GO-BI love the outcast. I thought I would offer this idea to Bill, as a method of accepting.

'When you can't bear to be near her, what is it that's keeping you away?'

'I can't bear the sight of her. But she's my wife. I don't want her to be like that'.

I asked him to close his eyes – which he did - and try to form a picture of her when she was in her revolting state. His eyes snapped open again: 'I can't do that'.

'Try'

'OK. If you insist.' I let that pass.

'Now you have a choice. You can either walk away and pretend that's not Isobel and she doesn't have a drink problem, or you can go towards your wife who is revoltingly drunk and put your arms around her. The choice is yours'. A very tough choice.

Intense silence filled the room for some time before he relaxed a little and I asked: 'What's happening now?'

'I'm holding her'. Wonderful.

'And?'

'She's crying'. Then: 'Oh, Isobel, I'm so sorry. I haven't helped you'.

That was the breakthrough Bill needed. He had deeply accepted Isobel's problem and he was beginning to think that he could help them both move forward. In a very real sense he had Gone Out to and Brought In the horrible idea that Isobel was an alcoholic, and had made it part of himself. He was not trying to pretend it didn't exist any more: he had accepted the fact. I thought he was alone with his thoughts but then I realized he was talking, very softly, to her. I just caught the words: 'I love you, Bella'.

Those are the moments when tears of gratitude and awe come to my eyes for the wonder of GO-BI loving.

Being Complacent

Being complacent is another way of trying to get out of accepting. It is saying: 'I don't like it but I don't need to do anything about it'. What we are being complacent about is most often something about ourselves that we wish was not so, because we are ashamed of it. Shame is a self-distancing emotion so it is an obstacle to GO-BI loving. Isobel was being complacent about her drinking. She didn't have the courage, the energy or the will power to change it. She was kidding herself that it wasn't a problem, or she laughed when she fell about a bit. She became able, with Bill's help, to say: 'It is so. I do drink too much'. That freed her to do something about it.

Resignation

For Bill the accepting he needed to do was of the fact: Isobel drank too much. For Tessa, who had come to me because she was depressed, it was slightly different. Her husband was always having a go at her. No matter what she did he always picked on her for little things: the house was not tidy; the dog needed grooming; his meal was not ready and he would miss the start of the football. She told me that she felt like a football herself sometimes, the number of times she got kicked. She also said: 'But there's nothing I can do about it, so I just have to put up with it'. Tessa thought she had accepted her lot but she hadn't. She was resigned, not accepting, because she still had an emotional attachment to the way her husband was in the sense that she felt very strongly that she did not want him to be that way.

He was not an easy person to love but she had loved him when they first got together. He was fun and she had enjoyed being his girl and then his wife. But she didn't think she loved him now. His continual complaining hurt her. Accepting was the tool she needed to use before she could choose to love again, or to move on in some other way.

If she accepted and became able to say: 'That's the way he is. I don't like it but I don't need it to be any different in order to get on with my life', would that make any difference to the way she felt?

I have a saying: 'The pain is in the resistance', which means that if we stop resisting: refusing to accept what is, the pain goes away. I have observed in my own life that sometimes not 'wanting it to be so' is painful and at other times it is more a case of: 'Oh, well. So be it.' The difference lies in whether I have chosen 'it' – whatever 'it' is – or whether it has been forced on me. When I have chosen for it to be so, in other words have accepted that it is so, it feels OK – it's my choice after all. It is only when I don't want it to be so, but nevertheless it is, that it really hurts. The pain is in the not wanting, the resisting, rather than in the particular circumstance. For instance I could be annoyed to think I had lost a five pound note, but feel OK if I remembered I had given it to a charity. I would be five pounds poorer either way but in the first case I would not have chosen to be so whereas in the second I would.

Tessa, though she was resigned, was resisting the fact that her husband was as he was and it was that which was causing her pain and making her depressed. It was not OK for him to pick on her all the time. However the fact was that he did. If she could accept – stop resisting - she would not be in pain and might be able to find a way of living with the fact, but not , of course, condoning it.

I asked her to think of an animal to represent her husband when he was getting at her. She thought for a bit and then said:

'A Starling'. That surprised me a bit and I asked her why.

'Because Starlings keep on pecking at things and that's what Pete does. Peck, peck, peck. All the time'.

I gave her some plasticine and asked her to make a Starling.

When she had finished to her satisfaction and the bird was nestling in her hand I asked: 'Did you know that you were living with a pecking Starling?'

'No'.

'Does knowing that you live with a Starling whose nature it is to peck make any difference to the way you feel?'

'What difference should it make?' she snapped.

Then, looking at the model in her hand: 'I suppose it's what a Starling does. Pecking. It doesn't know any different. It's just the way it is'.

'So what does it feel like; living with a pecking Starling?'

She screwed up her face, flattened out her hand so the model nearly fell off and then said: 'I'd rather have a Robin that fed out of my hand but if a Starling is what I've got, that's the way it is', and she gently closed her hand around it.

'And Pete the Starling?' I asked.

'Well, if that's the way he is, then that's the way he is. I wonder if I could train him to peck out of my hand instead of kicking me on the shins'. A sense of humour is a great healer.

Tessa, with the aid of a symbol, had accepted the Pete who pecked her, and was beginning to think what she might do about it.

I showed her the GO-BI loving doodles and explained about Going Out and Bringing In and that she could have Pete as a part of herself. She immediately realized that not wanting Pete to be the way he was was getting in the way of having him as part of herself: she did not want him within pecking distance. We worked on this for some time and then, during one session, I gave her back her plasticine Starling, which I had kept, and asked her to talk to it/Pete. She cradled it in both hands and looked at it: 'You're a picky, pecky, bastard and the daft thing is that I love you.'

By accepting the way Pete was, rather than merely being resigned, Tessa had been able to overcome the obstacle which had got in the way of her loving. She told Pete about the plasticine bird and, because her depression has lifted, she is now confident enough to say: 'Starling' to him when he is being particularly pecky. Life is not perfect in the Tessa-Pete household but has improved.

Giving In

I was out with a friend and I 'accepted' her suggestion to stop for coffee before finishing the shopping. I would have preferred to go on but I hadn't the guts to say: 'I'd rather get the shopping done before sitting down'. I didn't enjoy my coffee because I kept sneaking a look at my watch: I was resisting the situation I had got myself into. I had not accepted in that I had not been able to say: 'This is the way it is', which would have freed me to enjoy my coffee. I had merely given in: I was still emotionally attached to the idea of getting the shopping finished. I felt niggled with Patsy and was not Going Out to her, nor Bringing her In as fully as I usually did.

It Doesn't Matter

'So what? I know it happened but it doesn't matter', is another way of denying reality. In this case we have accepted the fact: it is so, but we are still resisting the meaning or significance that it has for us. Accepting often has to take place on three different levels. We have to accept the fact: 'it is so' – my wife has a drink problem; we have to accept 'how it came to be so' – I am depressed because my husband picks on me; and we have to accept 'what it says to me about me', which is often the hardest part of all.

Long ago I acknowledged the fact that my father went away, leaving me alone with my mother and brother, when he was called up for service in World War II. I said: 'I know he went away. So what?' What I did not acknowledge to myself until very much later was that his going left me feeling abandoned, unloved and unlovable. I had been denying the meaning that the event had for me, how it made me feel, what it seemed to be saying to me, about me. It was easier to do that, than to face those intense feelings. I seriously did not want them to be so.

Techniques for Accepting

Visualizing – imagining embracing Isobel – or using a symbol – holding a plasticine bird - are both powerful ways of changing our attitude of mind from: 'I don't want this' to: 'This is the way it is and I don't need to resist it any more'. I used a third way to move myself from: 'I don't want to feel this way' to: 'I accept that I do have these feelings; they are a part of me'. I call this method Absorption because we absorb a message that we have been resisting into ourselves, to make ourselves whole again.

A useful way of looking at ourselves, our inside world, is to imagine that we are surrounded by a wall, beyond which is our outside world. Inside the wall are our body, emotions, mind and spirit, and, right in the middle, our essential self: our 'I': the place we find when we do the meditation exercise I described in the section on Capacity For Awareness on p35. Facts about our outside world are like messages coming in to our inside world. If we don't like what the message says; if we want to resist it, we stuff it into some out of the way corner of ourselves and try to forget about it, much as we hide that difficult-to-deal-with letter at the back of our desk drawer.

I have found it helpful to understand the way these messages get into our heads. My father left home to serve in the army. This was the factual message coming in from my outside world. However I, like most children, was Self-focused so I processed that message to make it say something about me. I turned 'Daddy's gone' – which was an outside world fact – into: 'Daddy doesn't love me any more' – which was an inside world interpretation. That was such an awful thought that I needed it to have a reason: 'It must be because I am unlovable'. Then I found I simply could not handle such a painful message. I needed to get rid of it somehow: to cut off that excruciating part of me, so I put it in the not-to-be-remembered box at the back of my mind. It stayed there until one day I lifted the lid of the box, looking for something else as it happened, and out it popped.

I had been thinking, sadly, about how my relationship with my father had not been very close. I had always assumed that this was because he was not there during those crucial 0 – 7 years. I was sitting on the floor, where I usually do my thinking, when a picture came into my head of very young arms stretching out and I had a sense of crying: 'Don't go. Don't go'. My stomach knotted. I felt sick. Something truly terrible was happening.

I have no means of knowing for sure, but I believe this to be a memory of Father's departure when I was about eighteen months old. I knew, as part of family history, about the facts but I had buried the horrible feelings, and what the event said to me about me – 'I am unlovable' - in my not-to-be-remembered box, where it had remained. I had accepted the outside world fact: it was so, but I had hived off the feelings and how I had interpreted them. It was now, clearly, time I accepted at these two further levels: the feelings that I have and what it says to me about me.

First I needed to spend some time allowing myself to feel those feelings. What kept coming up was a sense that I wouldn't survive if Daddy went away and left me. There was no-one I could trust to keep me safe. But he had gone away. My world would never be the same again. Sitting on the floor in my adult body my child self howled and pleaded with him not to go, but it didn't make any difference. He didn't take any notice. He left. It felt as though something in me had died.

Now that I had remembered I had to do something with the memory if I didn't want to go on re-feeling those feelings. Our not-to-be-remembered box is a bit like Pandora's; you can't put things back in once they have got out. The problem that the feelings generated seemed to be what my father's departure said to me about me; the message it sent me from the outside world, so the Absorption technique seemed the obvious one to use. I put it off for quite a long while but eventually, one Saturday morning, I got down to it. I first needed to decide what the message really did say. 'I'm unlovable' seemed the obvious one but the more I thought about it the clearer it became that what it said was: 'I'm not worth it'. That rang true: 'I'm such utter rubbish that I'm not worth staying for'. This was the message that I was resisting having as part of myself. If I accepted it, acknowledged it as part of me, I would not be saying: 'It's true – you are not worth staying for'. I would be saying: 'Yes that message is part of who I am'. I would be accepting the *message* as a fact, not the *content* as truth. That seemed possible – and logical; I did have that message in my head; there was no getting away from the fact.

I set myself to imagine Going Out to the message I had parked in out of the way corner of myself, looping around it, and Bringing it In to the very centre of myself so it became part of what I am. I didn't want to do it; it was a struggle, but eventually I became aware of myself saying to myself: 'It's a message. It's been there all along. You have been resisting it – even though you thought you didn't know it was there – and that has caused you untold pain. It is a part of you, of your story. Accept that part of you'. I felt a warmth, something like when I am consciously GO-BI loving, and a sense that it was OK to have that message as part of myself. By accepting I had made the message accept-able. I had separated out the fact of the message from the truth of its content. The fact was acceptable - and true. I had harboured that message in the back of my mind since I was very small.

I was still left with the content: the belief that: 'I am not worth it', but now that I had accepted that it was there I could do something about it. We often need to use more than one tool to free ourselves from all the ramifications of a single incident. I had to choose whether the belief was true or not. I decided it was not so I used the tool of letting go to get rid of the false belief that I had held on to for so long.

Whatever method we use to arrive at accepting, when we have done it, we find that the thing we have been resisting and finding totally unacceptable has suddenly become acceptable; we know because we have just accepted it. And, because we are no longer resisting that it is so, we are no longer in pain. We feel strong enough to Go Out to and to Bring In ourselves and other people.

Chapter 10

Facing Down Fear

The Opposite of Love

There is some argument as to whether fear or hate, or even indifference, is the opposite of loving. One thing, however, is certain: fear is an obstacle to GO-BI loving. If we are afraid of being hurt, or of hurting someone else, we are not going to Go Out far enough for the damage to be done. If we are afraid of being taken over, or of being found wanting, we are not going to Bring In and lay ourselves open to being hurt. Fear, in any of its forms, is a serious obstacle to GO-BI loving.

Working With Facing Down Fear

I counselled Chris who was afraid that if he didn't please his father he would be rejected and ignored by him. Chris was highly intelligent and good at athletics, but hopeless at ball games. His father was a cricket fanatic and he wanted his son to be in the school First XI. Chris had never admitted to his father that he was in the no-hopers set for cricket, so he used to dread coming home and being asked: 'Have you been chosen for the First XI yet?' When he had to reply: 'No', his father used to say: 'I don't know what I've done to deserve such a useless son'. Chris desperately wanted to please his Dad but in the matter of cricket it simply was not in his power.

This caused him so much pain that he invented a fantasy world, and some fantasy behaviours, into which he could retreat. It was a form of flight from his fear of rejection and it worked so well that he came to prefer his fantasy world and the things he did in it, to the real one. He was a bit lonely because there weren't any other children in his fantasy world, but as a solution to the problem with his Dad it did the job admirably. His troubles began when he became an adult. Whenever he felt under pressure, especially from his boss at work, he could not help himself from resorting to his childhood behaviours.

He went to a psychiatrist who diagnosed him as having an incurable obsessive-compulsive disorder and told him he would just have to learn to live with it. Part of his difficulty was that he was so ashamed of his unacceptable behaviour that he couldn't make relationships, especially with women. He dared not run the risk of anyone finding out what he did. The psychiatrist's answer to this part of his problem was to recommend a visit to the local red light district, where the girls wouldn't mind. It was his inability to form relationships that made Chris come to see me, feeling depressed and desperately lonely.

As we explored his life, we saw clearly the sequence: fear of rejection by Dad → running away into fantasy → 'unacceptable' behaviours → shame → inability to form close relationships or to love. Underneath the shame was the fear that his behaviour would be seen as unacceptable if he let anyone close enough to find out about it, so he could not Go Out, neither could he Bring In. To unpack all of this we needed to start at the beginning with his fear of his Dad's disapproval.

Every summer afternoon that Chris walked home from school still not having made it to the First XI, he was afraid – in the 'now'. From past experience of his father making hurtful remarks about his useless son, Chris's future expectation was that he would do the same again when he got home. The walk home – the space between past experience and future expectation - was full of fear.

The same thing was happening at work now. When his boss asked him for something he wasn't sure he could do, Chris felt the same griping fear and wanted to switch into his fantasy world to relieve the stress. Fighting this was making him tired and depressed. The only way he would be able to have the courage to come out of his safe pretend-place and operate in the real world would be to face the original fear of being useless in his Dad's eyes, with all that said to him about him.

Facing Down Fear in Practice

The first thing we have to do if we want to deal with a fear is to identify it. It took Chris some time to come to understand that his fantasy world was his way of escaping from the fear of the pain of being a disappointment to his Dad. In a sense he had been running away from his Dad most of his life. What had been a relatively harmless childhood strategy was now costing Chris the ability to love his Dad, whom he admired, and his ability to live a full adult life, to form full adult relationships. It was time to face down his fear.

Facing down fear can be done by making a series of decisions. To start with I asked Chris if he wanted to stop running away from his Dad's disappointment. He said: 'Yes'. That was the first decision made. There's no point in even trying to change our mind or our behaviour if, deep down, we don't want to. Chris had a significant investment in staying the way he was. Though it had its down side, it was his place of safety and had served him well thus far. It was a big decision to choose to change.

I asked Chris to talk, out loud, to the father who inhabited his inside world and to tell him how afraid young Chris had been of not measuring up, and what he had done to escape that fear, and what that running away had cost him in terms of the way in which he was having to live his life now. This was painful and he found himself saying things he was not aware that he thought, but they were very real. When I judged he had got the particular pain of being a disappointment to his Dad out of his system, he was ready to make the second decision: to choose to turn and face his Dad. This was hard because it was breaking the habit of a lifetime.

He had already been 'talking to' his Dad but this second

decision meant that Chris really had to face him: to look him in the eye and say: 'I am not going to run away any more'. I encouraged him to repeat this, several times, until he was using his own words, rather than mine, and getting quite angry with his Dad. Eventually he said: 'I'm not going to run away from you just because I can't play cricket. I'm not going to go on being afraid of you for the rest of my life. I'm done with that'. That showed that the second decision was well and truly made.

He was now ready for the third decision: to challenge his Dad: 'If you want to say you 'don't know what you have done to deserve such a useless son', then say it.'

'If you want to reject me because I can't measure up to your standards, then that is what you will have to do'.

'Being afraid of you has cost me too much.'

'I haven't even got a girl friend let alone a wife.'

'I'm good at my job but I spend most of my time waiting to get something wrong.'

'I feel awful all the time and I'm not going to live like this any more.'

Chris was getting angry now which always gives energy to face a fear so I felt he would be able to issue the definitive challenge and tell his Dad to say: 'You are useless' and to say it now. When we are trying to make any hard decision there is a lot to be said for giving ourselves a decisive moment after which we know the change has taken place : 'Now I'm still dithering: Now I have decided'.

Chris hesitated for a second and then said: 'Dad, I'm fed up with being afraid that you will say I'm a useless son. I'm standing here and if you want to say it again to my face, then say it, and say it now!'

We were held in a powerful silence. I waited. Then I saw his face relax, so I asked: 'What's happening now?'

'Nothing. He hasn't said anything. He's just looking at me'.

This reply and his relaxed body told me that he was no longer afraid of the Dad in his head: he was no longer expecting to be told he was useless. If he had been, the reply would have been something more like: 'He's looking cross', or 'He said: 'I don't know what I did to deserve such a useless son' again, and I would have known there was more work to be done.

As the purpose of facing down our fears is to enable us to Go Out and to Bring In more fully, there was one more thing I wanted to do with Chris. I asked him to look into his father's eyes and tell me what he saw. He was very still for quite a time and then said: 'It's OK. He's smiling'.

I asked Chris if there was anything else he wanted to say to his Dad. A slight pause and then: 'I love you, Dad'.

I have been doing this sort of work for years now but it never ceases to amaze me how deeply people can enter into what might reasonably be called a charade, and emerge changed. When we deeply re-live an experience, but are at the same time conscious that it is not really happening now, we give ourselves an opportunity to re-write the ending. The original one has been affecting us all our lives: by changing it we change the meaning of the message we received so the content of the 'Shall I? Shan't I?' debate within ourselves changes and we are able to act differently in future. It also continues to astound me how brave people can be in facing down their fear of past abusers or future horrors like progressive illness. Chris had never before dared to give himself to his father; neither had he been able to Bring him In. His fear had made him keep his Dad at a distance. He had never GO-BI loved his Dad before.

Chris felt more relaxed the next time he saw his father. They talked about common interests and then Chris's job and a new project he was about to start. His Dad said: 'I'm proud of you son'. Chris told me that he nearly cried and wanted to hug him – but didn't. Next time perhaps.

The behaviours that Chris had originally devised as a way of coping with his fear, and which caused him so much shame, were no longer needed: he simply did not feel the urge to do them any more. He discovered he was able to create relationships and, in the fullness of time, a Mutual GO-BI loving.

What Are We Doing When We Face Down Fear

Fear is always about a future expectation. The difficulty is that, because the expectation is in our minds now so is the fear, even though the feared thing hasn't happened yet. Fear fills the whole of the space between the now, when we are thinking about 'it', and the future, when 'it' happens. It is the space harbouring the fear that causes us the problem. By making the three decisions - I don't want to be afraid anymore; I am not going to run away any more; I challenge you, Dad, to be disappointed in me and call me useless: 'Now!' - Chris had gradually squeezed the future expectation and the now together so there was no space left for the fear.

This may all sound rather fantastic playing around with ideas but remember it is all happening in our inside world. It worked for Chris and it has worked for many others, including myself. The psychological rationale for the technique is successive approximation: bringing the thing we fear nearer and nearer - the nurse's needle; the barking dog - until we are face to face with it and the space for being afraid in has gone. We have to cope - now. When, still in our inside world, the dreaded thing does not happen it shows that we have broken its emotional hold over us. Something similar may happen again in our outside world: we will have another injection; we will meet another fierce-sounding dog; someone may call us 'useless'. However, we will not have to react with stored up fear; we will be free to act appropriately.

Warnings

Two words of warning are necessary about facing down fear in this way. One; if the feared thing does happen in our inside world, this tells us that the space has not quite been squeezed out of existence: we are still a bit afraid. This does not mean that what has been done was invalid. It merely means that some aspect of the expected event has not been acknowledged; some part of the fear has not yet been faced. We need to identify this additional fear and then go through the three decisions to face it down.

The second warning is that the 'challenge and then it doesn't happen' scenario only applies in our inside world. We are in control of everything that happens in our inside world: we decide what goes on there. We do not have the same control over people or events in our outside world. It is not sensible to issue the: 'Do your worst' challenge to a drunken husband who is about to hit us. However, and this is the fascinating thing, if previously we have been able to deal with the fear of being hit, in our inside world, we might be able to influence what happens in our outside world. 'Don't do it' said fearlessly, and contrary to what he expects, will probably make him hesitate and give us time to get safe. While we are still afraid, even if we managed to say: 'Don't do it', the words would come out in a: 'But I expect you will' sort of voice, which would cancel out the power of the words themselves.

Chapter 11

Letting Go

Choice and Change

Deciding to do one thing rather than another involves choice. When we have chosen, we have to let go of that which we have not chosen. It may be letting go of an ideal vision of a person, or it may be a dream, or someone who is no longer alive, or a belief about ourselves. Loss and consequent change, because life will be different without whatever it is we were holding on to, are part of letting go. This is why letting go can be so scary: it is always a step into the unknown. We don't really know how we will cope in the new situation we will find ourselves in after we have let go. If we need to be in a new situation in order to be able to GO-BI love then staying stuck in the old place will be a serious obstacle to getting where we want to go.

Letting Go of an Ideal Person

Derek had been stuck holding on to a beautiful picture of his young wife. She was slim and lively, they had a lot of fun together and he loved her very much. Then, after some years, they hit a bad patch and she became depressed and put on a lot of weight. Derek desperately wanted to go on loving her, but was finding her more and more repulsive. This made him deeply ashamed, so he came to me for help. In exploring how he felt, we discovered he was still in love with the young girl he had married. He could not move on to a mature GO-BI loving of his real now-wife because he was stuck in a fantasy based on the past. We talked about what he found so horrible about Maggie as she was now and, though he didn't like the rolls of fat, what really upset him was that she was not as she had been. He had a momentous struggle even to decide to want to love her as she was now.

I asked him to make two cut-out figures representing the then-Maggie and the now-Maggie. When he had done it, I invited him to put then-Maggie on top of now-Maggie and asked: 'Who can you see?'

'Then-Maggie'

'What's happened to now-Maggie?'

'She's behind then-Maggie. She's hidden.'

'So?'

He took the point that he could no longer see his real now-wife because she was obscured by the fantasy one. 'Put them side by side so that you can see them both. Now talk to each of them. Tell them how you feel about living with them.'

He reminisced about the fun he and then-Maggie had had: the walking holidays and the tennis tournaments, and the all night-parties. Then he looked up and said: 'But I wouldn't want all that now.'

'Talk to now-Maggie.'

'Maggie, I don't know what's happened. Where did we get lost? Then-Maggie was a lot of fun but it was you who kept us afloat when I was out of a job. It was you who kept everything together when I was ill. It is you I talk to about problems at work. But I want to hold then-Maggie. She's the one I want to make love to. That sounds terrible, but it's the truth. It's the way I feel.'

'There's your choice then, Derek. Who do you want to live with? Who do you want to love?' Again a tough choice but enormously empowering.

He struggled with himself because he wanted them both; but he couldn't GO-BI love now-Maggie while he was longing for the other one. He knew he had to choose one and let go of the other. He was holding the two pictures, one in either hand; looking from one to the other. Suddenly his right fist clenched, crushing then-Maggie: 'You're in the way. You've had your time. I'm finished with you.' He let then-Maggie drop to the floor.

If he had violently thrown her away I would have been concerned that he still had an emotional attachment to her – anger probably. Simply opening his hand and allowing her to fall was a real letting go.

'Talk to now-Maggie', I said.

'Maggie I'm sorry. You're still the same you. If you look like a stranded whale, that's OK. Remember how excited we were whale spotting off British Columbia? I love whales. I love you, Mags: just as you are'.

Letting go of the fantasy wife from the past had enabled Derek to GO-BI love his real, now, wife Maggie; just as she is.

Letting Go of a Dream Self

Something similar happened to Kirsty, only her problem was that she had a dream of what she might be. This was preventing her from Going Out to and Bringing In the Kirsty she was now.

She had always dreamed of being a painter but, in fact, she taught art in a rundown inner city school. This felt such a come down that she was not able to put her heart into it. She needed to let go of her dream in order to engage with the reality which was that she could make an wonderful difference to the lives of deprived children by giving them a sense of achievement: by valuing their work/them; by loving them.

We discovered that being a painter, for Kirsty, meant earning her living by it. That was the image she needed to let go: she didn't have to cut painting out of her life. We had to think carefully how to make the distinction between being a painter and painting. At just the right time in our exploration she received an invitation to the private view of a friend's exhibition. The stylish card was an ideal symbol for her own image of being a painter.

There are many ways of letting go of such symbols: tearing up; putting in the bin; flushing down the loo; burying in the garden. Kirsty chose to burn hers. As the last sparks died in the ashes she released a big sigh. It felt like a significant letting go.

We worked together for a while longer on other issues so she was later able to tell me how her teaching was going. She was finding that, without the conflict between being a painter and being a teacher of painting, she was able to put more of herself into her class work – to Go Out – and to see more of value in the children and their efforts – to Bring them In. Her dream self had been getting in the way of her GO-BI loving her students. When the dreaded Ofsted inspection came round, hers was one of the best reports in the school.

Letting Go of a Loved One

Sometimes we have to let go of a loved one in order to free ourselves to love again. Alex came to me because he was having trouble maintaining relationships. He was an attractive man and had no difficulty in acquiring girlfriends. All went well for a while but when they began to become committed to each other he would pick a fight and withdraw. For a long time he managed by believing it was always the girl's fault but then a brave and true friend took him aside, pointed out what was happening, and suggested he seek help.

As we explored his life it emerged that he had been deeply in love with Gill eight years before. They had been on holiday together when she fell violently for one of the other men in their group. They were engaged within a month. Alex was devastated. What he had not realized was that every time he became close to another girl Gill got in the way. The new girl was not Gill and he could not bear it. We talked about how holding on to a past love can be an obstacle to loving again and he came to see how that was happening in his life.

I like the phrase 'carrying a candle' for someone, meaning we love them, so I asked Alex if 'carrying a candle' for Gill resonated with him. His face brightened: 'Yes. I like that idea'. I keep a candle at the ready so I lit it and placed it on the table beside Alex.

'You have been carrying that flame for Gill for eight years now. It is getting in the way of you creating another deep relationship. What do you think you could do about it?'

He gave the obvious answer: 'Blow it out'. Then he added: 'But I don't want to lose her. She is part of me'.

'Tell her that. Talk to the flame and tell her how much she means to you.'

Alex talked to her for quite a while and then said: 'But you're not mine any more. You chose Drew. I can't go on waiting for you. I need to move on. If that means letting you go, I suppose that is what I will have to do. But I don't know how to.'

'Like you said, you could blow out that candle flame. It will be hard but you can choose to do it.'

Alex stared into the flame as if his eyes would devour it. Time passed. He squared his shoulders; blew; and then watched as the smoke dispersed. 'She's gone', he said with a sigh – always a sign that something significant has happened: that tension has been released.

Doing this sort of thing is effective because it engages the whole of ourselves body, emotions, mind and spirit, in making the change.

Bereavement

In bereavement, although we know our beloved has gone from our outside world, we hang on to wanting them in our inside world. We cannot love again until we have let them go but sometimes we confuse letting go with forgetting – and we don't want to do that - so we stay stuck. We don't have to let go of all that we already have of them. That can never be taken away, unless we choose to forget. We can go on loving them to the end of our days. What we need to let go of is the wanting more of them day by day. We need to let go of the 'I want us to be the way we were'. If we can do that we can keep our beloved's special GO-BI loving loop but, because we have let go of wanting them now, we become free to make a new loop for someone else as well.

Kirsty burned her invitation as a way of letting go; Alex blew out a candle. Another way of letting go is to use visualization. We can imagine leaving our beloved by walking away ourselves, or we can let them walk away from us. I let my father go, after he had died, by watching him, in my mind, walk away from me, across his garden and then he simply kept on walking out across the city until I couldn't see him any more. There wasn't a decisive moment like there was for Kirsty or Alex but I definitely knew when he had gone. It was a bit like when the last note of a symphony is finally no longer there and the silence is total. It was a beautiful and healing moment.

Letting Go of a Self-Belief

If we have a deep belief about ourselves, for instance that we are unlovable, it simply does not help to tell ourselves; 'No you're not. Lots of people love you'. Susan found herself in this position so I used what I call the Thought Bubble Technique to help her see what was going on for her. I drew a pin-person with a balloon coming out of her head and asked Susan to write in it what she believed about herself. She wrote: 'I am unlovable'.

'Is that really true?' I asked

'Well, I know some people love me but I still know I'm unlovable'

We looked at the doodle for a bit then I asked her to write round the Thought Bubble a few of the 'I love you' messages that she knew were out there. When she had done that I added arrows from the words to the edge of the Thought Bubble.

'What's happening now?'

'They've stopped. They can't get in'.

We talked about how the 'I'm unlovable' thought was keeping out any other thought that didn't agree with it. It simply is not possible to believe other people's thoughts if we have a contrary one firmly embedded in our mind. Interestingly, the more insecure we are in ourselves the more tenaciously we hold on to our self-beliefs.

'Is the 'I am unlovable' message truth or a lie?' I asked.

'The truth' she replied firmly. 'Though I know it's a lie as well'.

We needed to spend some time on this, exploring where the belief came from and what had been the effect on her life of believing it. The more we talked the more she realized how that thought coloured everything she did. It was also was preventing her Going Out and Bringing In because she absolutely did not believe that she could love or be loved. In a subsequent session, she got so angry that she decided it must be a lie.

'So, what is the Truth?' I asked. Long pause.

'I am I lovable', I suppose'.

I then invited her to rub out the lie in her Thought Bubble and substitute it with the truth. This was hard and she did it very slowly and thoughtfully but, I was pleased to see, she put a very definite full stop after the 'I am lovable'. She had instinctively given herself a decisive moment. She looked up and smiled.

We talked about being love-able, and that, if she chose, she could take the initiative in Going Out and Bringing In. She could make herself into a loving person and, I explained, it is in loving that we feel loved. Susan had many fears and wrong beliefs about herself which made it hard for to Go Out and to Bring In but at least she had over come one obstacle and she had begun to GO-BI love herself.

Chapter 12

Forgiving

Who Benefits?

In a psychological sense, as distinct from a theological or a moral one, forgiving is primarily for our own benefit because it frees us from the burden of grievance that keeps us at a distance from those we want to GO-BI love. Our burden of grievance is made up of pain, physical, emotional, or both, and anger, directed at another or ourselves. It works like this: someone ran into me with their shopping trolley:

Pain [It hurt my leg] + Anger [I'm cross they didn't care] = I feel aggrieved.

I may simply shrug it off as 'one of those things' but if I dwell on it I get stuck in a pain → anger → grievance → pain-in-remembering cycle, which can be highly corrosive.

Forgiving does not alter the facts: what happened happened, and it was not alright. What forgiving does is take the pain out of remembering, which then breaks the grievance cycle. We cannot Go Out to nor can we Bring In anyone, including ourselves, who causes us pain. Remembering is like picking at a scab until the wound bleeds again. When we forgive we bind up the wound so that it really heals; we let go of the grievance and release ourselves from the pain-in-remembering.

Trying to Go Out to, or to Bring In the person who has hurt us will inevitably remind us of our grievance. If remembering is painful, then Going Out or Bringing In will seem like a bad idea. If we want to be able to GO-BI love the only answer is to take the pain out of the remembering. This, as far as I know, can only be done by forgiving.

The FEE Model

The depth of our forgiving is directly proportional to the accuracy with which we assess what has to be forgiven. Forgiving is often thought of in terms of writing off a debt. Using the accounting idea gives us a model for finding out precisely what we are owed. We can draw up an account, an invoice, against the person we feel owes us. We can put on it the Facts: what actually happened, our Emotions: what we felt at the time, and the Effects on our life at the time and since. I call this the FEE Model: it helps us to know exactly what the debt is that we are owed: what is our grievance.

After the supermarket incident I took a piece of paper, wrote 'Invoice' at the top, and drew up an account against the person who ran into me with their trolley. This is how it looked:

INVOICE

To: Person Unknown in Supermarket

Facts:	ran over my foot with trolley	xxx
	it hurt	xxx
	it laddered my tights	xxx
Emotions:	angry	xxx
	felt ignored	xxx
	not noticed	xxx
Effects:	grumpy to check-out girl	xxx
	ignored a friend I saw in the street	xxx
Total:		<u>xxxx</u>

When I had done it I was surprised how emotionally hurt I had felt: remembering the incident, trivial though it was, brought back the pain. I now had an accurate measure of my grievance. I also had something tangible to work with in writing off what I felt I was owed. There are lots of ways we can choose to involve our body, emotions, mind, and spirit in cancelling a debt. I chose to tear up my invoice and put it in the bin. I then felt free of the nastiness inside which had made me unable to GO-BI love the check-out girl or the friend I saw in the street afterwards.

Forgiving Others

Dealing with Anger

Being angry: 'Why should I forgive the bastard?' gets in the way of forgiving. We don't want to forgive while we are still angry. If the anger is the long held-on-to, smouldering, sort it can become so much part of who we think we are that it is very hard to shift. We may not want to let it go because it has become part of our identity. We may also confuse ceasing to be angry with saying it was OK – when it most definitely wasn't – but, if that is how we think, we feel compelled to hang on to our anger. When we are in either of these positions we usually need to deal with the anger before we can even think about forgiving.

I have recently worked with Sheila, who was hideously sexually abused by her father when she was a child. It was over a long period but there was one incident, when she was quite small, that was particularly horrific. There are people who think that forgiving is not possible in such circumstances, but I am not one of them. Sheila, and many others, justify my belief. Some therapists believe they do not have the right to ask their Counsellees to forgive such horrendous things. I believe that I do not have the right not to offer someone who has come to me for help the chance to let go of such a terrible burden of grievance and to remove an obstacle to their GO-BI loving. I don't believe in letting them tip over into completely re-living their agony, nevertheless it takes all my courage to lead someone to approach it and them all their courage to follow.

Sheila, as others like her, was aware of the pain of her father's betrayal but her anger was still hidden from her, so it might have seemed that the first thing to do was to work through forgiving. However, she did not want to forgive and that was because, deep down, she was murderously angry. The anger needed to be got out of the way first.

Her anger was partly the bewildered: 'How could you?' sort, and partly an intense desire for revenge: 'I'd like to hurt you as much as you hurt me'. She did not want to believe herself capable of such violent feeling: it was both frightening and shaming. For Sheila, as for most of us, it was more acceptable to feel hurt than to feel angry: to be a victim rather than a perpetrator. This was why she was hiding her anger from herself.

Using The FEE Model

I knew Sheila was full of hatred – how could she not be? – but she was more aware of her hurt so we started working on that. Over many weeks we drew up a list of the Facts: what had actually happened. We drew up another of the Emotions she felt at the time, and a final one of the Effects of what had happened in her life afterwards. It was the final list, the effects, which brought out Sheila's anger. She came face to face with the enormous cost in self-loathing, lack of trust in men, and the total impossibility of giving herself to anyone, much less of bringing anyone in to herself. She now knew why she had felt all her life that she was not fit to exist. She was raging.

Anger has physical manifestations, trembling, sweating, and knotting of muscles which is probably why most people, and Sheila was no exception, have surprisingly little difficulty in imagining it as being in a particular part of their body. They can picture it as having a shape, substance, texture or colour, which make it seem a tangible object that can be got hold of. This provides a useful way of working with it, involving the whole person: the body, as well as the emotions, mind and spirit.

I asked Sheila what her anger looked like; and where it was in her body.

'It's a black lump', she said and ground her fists into the pit of her stomach.

'Can you get your hands around it?' She dug her fingers into her tummy and said: 'Mmm'.

'Now, try to pull it up through your body, slowly and carefully. Then throw it out of the top of your head. It will be very hard, it has been there a long time, so pull with all your might.'

She locked her fingers, tensed her arms, and started to draw her hands upwards.

'Keep going. Keep pulling. It's really hard to shift. Keep a hold of it. Don't stop.' I urged her on.

She got red in the face and was holding her breath and then, with a final surge of energy, she threw her arms above her head, unclenched her fists and, spreading her fingers wide, thrust her hands forward in a very clear flinging away gesture. She flopped forward and let out a huge sigh. The release was proportionate to the amount of effort she had put in.

Sheila was exhausted so I kept quiet until she sat up straight again and then I said: 'Look around inside, where that black lump was, and see if any bits got left behind.' It is always useful to do this check because it is easier to go back at the time than in a subsequent session.

She closed her eyes and was very still. Then: 'No. It's all gone'.

'How do you feel?'

'Shattered. Lighter. Phew!' And then: 'What was all that about?'

'Well, by visualizing your anger you made it tangible. The black lump became your hatred of your Dad. You attached all your fierce emotion to it. Putting all that effort into heaving it out by the longest possible route engaged the whole of you; body, emotions, mind and spirit. The release was telling the whole of you that the emotion was no longer part of you.'

Writing Off the Debt

At the beginning of the next session I asked Sheila if she had
found herself behaving any differently since our last meeting.

'Not especially' she said. Then added: 'But my father-in-law
was less tiresome than usual.'

'Was he different or were you able to tolerate his tiresomeness
more easily?'

'Oh. I see. I'm the one who was different: not such an angry
person. Is that it?'

I looked at her and smiled. 'Could be'.

'So now you are no longer angry with your Dad for that
particular thing, we can start working on forgiving him'.

'But I can never forget what he did.'

This is a common misapprehension: that forgiving is about
forgetting. It's not. Forgiving takes the pain out of remembering.
Forgiving breaks the cycle of pain → anger → grievance → pain-
in- remembering.

Having reassured Sheila on that one, and that, by forgiving,
she would not be saying that what her Dad did was OK, or didn't
matter, I went on to explain the idea of forgiving as cancelling a
debt. As long as we feel we are owed something we will feel
aggrieved that we have not been paid. There are many debts that
cannot, or will not, be paid. The debtor may not be aware of the
debt or he may now be dead. I may think my friend Mary-Jane
owes me but she is convinced that she does not, so she is never
going to pay up. A visitor broke a mug that my father had given
me. She bought me another one but it wasn't Father's mug: it was
not possible to make full restitution. In my heart she still owed
me – and always would - until I chose to cancel the debt.

By absolutely not considering her personhood Sheila's father
had made her feel that she did not exist. That was the debt he
owed her and that was the debt she needed to write off if she was
to rid herself of her burden of grievance and all its consequences
that made her afraid, and therefore, unable to GO-BI love.

I explained: 'He can't take away the burden of grievance that you are carrying. The only way to release yourself from this terrible weight is to cancel the debt. This means that you will be letting him go free. You will be bearing the cost yourself, but', I added, 'you have been doing that all your life anyway'.

This is one of the really tough things about forgiving: it is the forgiver, the one who was hurt, who pays the price. It is the opposite of revenge which is trying to: 'Make the so-and-so pay for what he did'. If my friend owes me some money but I write off the debt, I am the one who is out of pocket. And, what is more, I am accepting to be out of pocket; I don't try sneaky ways of getting back at her.

Sheila had already done a Facts, Emotions, and Effects exercise to put her in touch with the anger she felt; what had happened, how she felt, and how it had affected her life from then on. We spent several sessions going over it again as a way of drawing up an invoice against her Dad. Sheila was going to have to talk to him so it was important to to have a clear, and defined idea of what she was going to say. When the time comes there is always a temptation to add in other bits: 'And then there was the time... And then there was that other time...' Forgiving like this is not so effective, not so releasing, because we can't deeply acknowledge too many grievances at once.

Keeping to what she had decided were the main points, though using spontaneous words, Sheila went over her 'invoice' and told her Dad how she felt and how what he had done had affected her. When I thought she had said all she needed to I asked her: 'Is there anything else he ought to know about that time?'

'I don't think so.' Then, more firmly: 'No'.

'Say to him: 'That's what you owe me. There's no way you can pay the debt you owe me. It happened and you can't make it un-happen'.

When she had done that I went on: 'Sheila, look deep down

inside yourself and if, from the bottom of your heart, you can say to your Dad: 'I forgive you', then say it. But if it isn't true, don't say it. That's perfectly OK.' It was important that Sheila should forgive because she wanted to, not because it would please me.

I held my breath and eventually she said: 'I forgive you, Dad, for what you did that night'. It was an awesome moment. When I felt the silence lose some of its intensity I asked her: 'What's your Dad doing now?'

'Looking at me; sort of puzzled'. That sounded promising so I went on: 'What would you like to do now?'

'Give him a hug', was the reply. I find it totally mind-blowing that this should happen, but it usually does. Apart from being deeply humbling, Sheila demonstrated that, once the obstacles of hatred and grievance were overcome, GO-BI loving was her natural response: that was what she had always wanted to do.

Forgiving Ourselves – Dealing with Guilt

Guilt is anger directed against ourselves. Forgiving ourselves has the same aim as forgiving other people: namely, to relieve ourselves of the burden of grievance, this time against ourselves. For most of us, however, self forgiving is harder than forgiving other people. We often feel, not simply that we have done something wrong which we regret, but that we are wrong to our very core, and are, therefore, unforgivable.

I worked with Roger on an issue of guilt. He had had an affair with a woman colleague at work. His wife, Anne, did not know about it and he hated himself for deceiving her. The affair came to an end and he thought he could simply put it all behind him and carry on as normal. This did not happen. He felt terrible and after some months was diagnosed as suffering from depression. Anne, of course, was worried but Roger could not tell her what the trouble was, nor that at times he felt he did not want to go on living. This continued for about a year and then he came to see me.

After we had talked for a while and got to know each other a little, we both realized how agonizingly guilty he felt about the affair, and that this was the probable cause of his depression. He felt he could never forgive himself for what he had done. It went against everything he valued about family life. He had transgressed his own deeply held code. Though he didn't know it, he had 'I am unforgivable' in his Thought Bubble.

I explained my understanding of forgiving to him. There was no possibility of him drawing up an account against himself, with a view to forgiving himself, while he had: 'I am unforgivable', in his Thought Bubble. The way round this was to start with what he thought that Anne would put on an account of his debt to her, if she knew what he had done. This suited his mood because he was full of self-recrimination.

Using the FEE Model again, the 'Facts' were simple. She would put: 'my husband had an affair with another woman'. Under 'Emotions' Roger thought she would put: 'I feel betrayed, he has rubbished our love. I feel sick, let down. He's a two-timing bastard', etc, etc. This list was long. On the 'Effects' one Roger thought Anne would put: 'I will never trust him again' and 'I don't feel close any more'.

This was interesting because one of the effects he was suffering, because guilt is a self-distancing emotion, was that he no longer felt close to her. What Roger had written down were his own feelings about himself, but it was easier for him to think that they were Anne's. By using projection in this way we were able to find out what he really thought and felt about himself. Everything on the account really belonged to him but he was not able to look at his own thoughts and feelings yet; they were still drowned in his over-whelming sense of misery and unforgivableness. Drawing up Anne's/his account helped him get in touch with his own feelings about having been unfaithful. Until he had done that he could not meaningfully cancel the debt he owed himself because he did not really know what it was. All he knew was that he felt awful, and believed that he could never forgive himself for what he had done.

Having drawn up Anne's/his account, which took several sessions, I invited Roger to picture her in his inside world, and to talk to her about what he owed her. He started off talking for her: 'You feel I betrayed you', but after a while he slipped into the first person singular: 'I'm a bastard'. He was acknowledging the thoughts and feelings as his own. I didn't comment on this change. He wasn't ready to forgive himself directly so he needed the safety of the projection. Instead I said: 'Tell Anne how you feel about it all'.

'I'm so desperately sorry. I would give anything for it not to have happened.'

'Can you ask Anne to forgive you?'

'How can she ever do that?'

'Do you think there is something else that she believes you owe her?'

Pause for thought: 'Yes. I eyed that blonde in the hotel on our honeymoon. You were furious'.

It often happens that we cannot put the words: 'I forgive you', even into someone else's mouth, while there is still something on our conscience. I suggested he tell Anne how he felt about that now, and then, to get a clear picture of her in his mind and to ask: 'Anne, will you forgive me'. He managed it this time.

I left a space before asking: 'What is Anne doing?'

'She's smiling'.

'And what is her smile saying?' I needed to be sure where he had got to.

'She has forgiven me'.

What had happened was that the 'I am unforgivable' message in his Thought Bubble had faded a bit. He still believed it but not quite as firmly as before: he had just accepted that he could be forgiven by Anne – who, in the work we were doing, was a part of himself. He had taken a step towards forgiving himself.

Most people believe in some Higher Power which is helpful when they come to forgiving themselves because it gives another step to the process. Roger believed in God so I next invited him to tell God all he felt he had done to Anne. When he had said it all, including the honeymoon bit, I suggested he ask God to forgive him. For some people this can be a very scary moment because their God is an angry father, but others believe in a loving God, so it is relatively easy. Roger was able to believe that his God opened his arms to him, and forgave him. Psychologically this was still a projection, whatever it might have been spiritually or theologically. Roger had again found himself forgivable and the contrary message in his Thought Bubble faded a bit more.

We had been getting Roger's mind used to the idea that he was forgivable. In his projections of Anne/Roger and God/Roger he had already forgiven himself. However I stuck with the projection a little longer because he had been so adamant that he could never forgive himself. I got tough and said: 'Anne and God, who you have hurt, have forgiven you. Do you still feel you are unforgivable?'

'I can't forgive myself for what I did.'

'But they can. Are you rubbishing their forgiving?'

This is hard but it usually helps people to see that they are hanging on to their un-forgiving of themselves, for no very good reason. I asked Roger to go through it all once more, this time talking to himself. The rationale behind this was to fade the message in his Thought Bubble even more.

When I judged he had said enough I prompted him to say: 'Roger, I forgive you,' but, I cautioned: 'only if it is true'.

He was silent for a while and then: 'Roger, I forgive you for your affair with Penny'.

This was another interesting snippet because it was the first time he had mentioned the other woman's name; he had finally and fully admitted to himself what had happened, and there was no pain in remembering her name. He had put 'I am forgiven' in his Thought Bubble and laid down the burden of grievance against himself. With it he let go of his depression. He was free to go back to GO-BI loving his wife.

I appreciate that this sounds like merely playing around in our imaginations but actually it is engaging different levels of our consciousness to help us change our mind about something buried deep within us. Most of us have experienced trying to change the way we think or feel about something – 'I'm not going to beat myself up about this any more' – and then, at three o'clock in the morning we find ourselves going over it all again and saying: 'What a fool I've been'. We sometimes need more than a good intention to help us bring about a change of mind. By going through all those stages Roger had gradually worked himself into a different frame of mind.

And what about Anne? She had never known about the affair but she had been worried about Roger. She was now delighted that he was no longer depressed, and she rejoiced in the restoration of their mutual loving. Should he tell her? I don't know. He was no longer carrying the burden of grievance against himself that made him distance himself from her. Their loving relationship was restored but it now had a secret in it. Time would tell whether this proved to be an obstacle to GO-BI loving. If it did, more forgiving would be needed; this time Anne would need to choose to forgive Roger on her own behalf.

Feeling Forgiven

It was only when Roger forgave himself: changed his thought from: 'I am unforgivable' to: 'I am forgiven' that he actually felt forgiven. Even if Anne had known about the affair and had forgiven him, that message would not have got through while he had: 'I am unforgivable' in his Thought Bubble. We always think we know best and if we feel unforgivable, then that's what we are, regardless of what anyone else may say. Psychologically we have to forgive ourselves before we can receive the forgiving of anyone else.

Misconceptions About Forgiving

Forgiving a serious grievance is not easy. It is made much harder by a number of misconceptions about 'forgiveness' – that noun again – which can get us off on the wrong tack or give us an excuse for not setting out on the process of forgiving at all. The most frequently found one, that I have already mentioned, is that forgiving is about forgetting. It is not. The purpose of forgiving is to take the pain out of remembering.

A number of other misconceptions about forgiving make it dependent on the other person doing something, which means that unless they do, we can't relieve ourselves of the burden of un-forgiveness. Similarly we do not have to involve the other person by admonishing them, the polite word for 'having it out', before we can forgive; it is our own angry feelings which are the obstacle to GO-BI loving and we need to deal with them inside ourselves, not project them onto the person we are angry with.

Theologically the forgiving process requires the repentance of the offender. It is a two-way process in which both parties have to be engaged. Psychologically we need not wait for the person who has offended us to say 'Sorry'. We can complete the process of shedding the burden of grievance, as Sheila did, on our own in much the same way as we can create a one-lover GO-BI loving.

Restitution, as in the case of Father's mug, cannot always be made, and even if it can, we are foolish to make it a condition for forgiving because we then make our healing dependent on someone else's action.

Lastly, forgiving and justice having been done are two separate things. The sentence meted out by a judge may be just in that the offender will pay the price the law requires, but that does not deal with the terrible pain in the hearts of the parents whose child has been killed. That sort of agony shuts off all desire to Go

Out or to Bring In: it can, and often does, become all-consuming. Only forgiving can release the flow of GO-BI loving again.

Both anger and guilt are self-distancing emotions so forgiving, which deals with both, enables us to re-build our broken side of the our-relationship. If I manage to forgive you before you have been able to deal with your guilt and forgive yourself, or vice versa, one of us will have to wait for the other before the our-relationship is restored. In the meanwhile the one who has got ahead is free to one-lover GO-BI love the one who is still struggling with their self-distancing emotion.

This way of forgiving, which takes place in our inside world, is not dependent on the other person's response – any more than GO-BI loving is dependent on the other person. However, this does not mean, as some people argue, that this intrapsychic forgiving is not about relationships. I believe that the purpose of forgiving is to relieve the pain of self-distancing emotions which are such obstacles to GO-BI loving. It is only when we have let go of a grievance against ourselves or someone else that we become free to GO-BI love ourselves or the other person.

Using The Whole Tool Kit

I have talked about using each of the four tools of Accepting, Letting Go, Facing Down Fear and Forgiving on their own. We can take the appropriate tool out of the box and apply it to the particular issue facing us, either in ourselves or somebody else. The tools help us to fill the gaps in our flow of Going Out and Bringing In. They help us to do more joined-up GO-BI loving.

There are, however, times when we have to take the whole kit to an issue because more than one tool will be needed before the problem is fully resolved. This is always the case with complex relationships like those with parents or spouses. There is never a single issue which, when resolved, means that everything is fine. In these relationships different facets of a single issue may need to be re-visited again and again, using a different tool each time.

This does not mean that the work that we did the first time round was in any way inadequate. It may mean simply, that by dealing with one pain, we uncover a deeper one underneath.

One of the incidents that gave me the message that my Mum did not love me happened when I was between two and three. She had a brother who was killed in World War II. I believe he was the person she loved most in the world. I don't know how she got the news, but I have a vivid picture of her sitting at her dressing table, with its blue enamel-backed brushes and hand mirror, sitting on a stool that he had given her. She has her head in her hands, and is sobbing. I go towards her, wanting to offer myself as comfort: to Go Out to her. She ignores me. There is nothing I can do to help. She does not want me. To hold me will not comfort her. I don't know how to Bring her In, so I stand bereft, feeling helpless.

I have gone back, time and again, to that scene. It took me a while to allow myself to re-feel the sense of total abandonment. My world, my life, had come to an abrupt halt. It was the second case of: 'Something died in me', in my short life. Nothing would ever be the same again. The only adult left in my world who I could rely on [Father having been called up about a year before] had effectively turned her back on me.

I never felt totally safe with her after that. I did not feel significant to her; my self-offering had been ignored; it was not acceptable to her. Feeling unimportant to her, I had an obscure sense that, if the chips were down, she would not keep me safe. Looking back as an adult, I realize that she was probably experiencing the same sense of the bottom having dropped out of her world that I was. I am sure something died in her too. I know that she always cherished a hope that her brother was not really dead but had been washed up on the coast of Norway. She was so totally immersed in her grief, that she may not even have been aware that I was standing there - I would have approached quietly, I am sure. It was a terrible time for both of us and neither of us knew how to Go Out to or to Bring In the other. A part of me clanged shut. I felt utterly worthless. Alone. Cut off from my mother. If I did not exist for her, how could I exist at all?

I have had to accept what happened and what it said to me about me. I have had to face the fear of not being safe and of not existing at all. I have had to let go of the dream of having a different sort of Mum: one who had more time for me. Lastly, and probably the hardest part, I have had to acknowledge that I was furiously angry and was carrying a huge burden of grievance at what I felt was the rejection of my proffered comfort. That needed forgiving. This one incident needed all the tools, more than once, but each time I used one I found myself able to GO-BI love my Mum not yet perfectly, but more fully.

Part 3

Chapter 13

Living GO-BI loving

Yes, But...

There is head knowledge; there is heart knowledge; and there is living knowledge. The head bit of GO-BI loving is easy: loving is Going Out from ourselves and Bringing In our intended beloved. The heart bit is harder but we may be able to imagine a Bringing In that fills the void, giving us the warmth of being loved. We may even conceive the possibility that we would not feel loved unless we were ourselves loving. However, when it comes to living GO-BI loving, there's always a: 'Yes, but...' We think we have got it and then the problems and the questions crop up and we realize that, though the GO-BI loving idea appears simple enough, we have to tear ourselves apart in order to do it. Living GO-BI loving requires a choice by the whole of us: body, emotions, mind and spirit, to enter fully into giving our deepest self and making our intended beloved part of ourselves.

Wanting To Be Loved

Zoe originally came to see me because her marriage to Ralph was not working. At various times she had used all the tools on different parts of that relationship and, though it was not perfect, she now felt much happier in it. However, she had come to realize that she had a very deep yearning for her Dad's love, although she had not had a good relationship with him when she was a child. She was wanting his love, but feeling that it was now too late, since he had died two years before.

We had talked about this before but I felt there were two

things she needed to look at again. One was that, though her Dad no longer existed in her outside world, she thought about him often: he was still very much alive in her inside world. This meant that she needed to heal whatever was still raw in her relationship with him there. The second was that she had: 'I want to be loved' in her Thought Bubble and this was keeping her stuck because she thought, as most of us do, that *being* loved was the only solution to wanting to *feel* loved. This was a 'Yes, but...' situation because, though she knew something about GO-BI loving, it obviously was not helping her with her father. We needed to look at the whole idea again.

I started off by asking her: 'What does being loved feel like?'

'I don't know.' Then: 'Having arms around us'. 'Warmth inside'. 'A glow filling us.'

'Mmm. Anything else?'

'Something, love I suppose, flowing in; filling the space inside.'

'Yes'. I said, 'I think those are all being-loved-type-feelings'.

'So, let's look at the GO-BI loving doodles again.' I got out my white board and started drawing. 'You are the little Green person and your Dad is the little Blue person'. You want to be loved by him: you want him to Go Out to you and to Bring you In to himself. You've been wanting that all your life. Right?'

'Yes. I guess so.'

'So, when the little Blue person, your Dad, Goes Out and Brings In the little Green person, you, he fetches up with the little Green person inside him, she is now part of him'. I had drawn the middle doodle on the front cover, only with Blue doing the GO-BI loving, not Green. I paused and then went on: 'Who is feeling warm? Who's inside space is being filled? Who has the being-loved-type-feelings?'

Zoe looked puzzled, as well she might: 'It seems to be the Blue one, Dad.'

Then she added: 'I thought I had got all this but obviously I haven't. Are you saying that it is the one who Goes Out and Brings In – the one who is loving - who has the being-loved-type-feelings?'

'Yes, that's exactly what I am saying. And not only me: there is an old Italian proverb quoted by the fifteenth century writer, Ficino: 'If you want to be loved [to feel loved] then love.'

'But supposing Dad, Blue, is loving me, why don't I feel it?'

'Look at the doodle again. Blue's loop is going around Green, with the idea of bringing her to himself: to become part of him. The energy of his loving, his loop, is not touching her; she's coming to him on it's flow of energy. She wants to be loved, but she's not feeling loved, because she is not open to it; she is not receiving it; she is not Bringing it In. And that is because she is not Going Out.'

I waited for her to catch up and then went on: 'If the little Green person [you] is doing the loving – Going Out and Bringing In the little Blue person – then the doodle looks like this' and I drew exactly the one on the front cover. It is Green who has the warm being-loved-type-feelings because she has Brought the little Blue person deep In to herself. The answer to wanting to be loved is for ourselves to be GO-BI loving.'

This is something similar the way relationships work. If you are aware of me but I am not aware of you I won't be aware of being aware your awareness of me either. I may think that you are ignoring me. It is only when I choose to be aware of you, which includes your awareness of me, that there can be an our-relationship: a connecting between us. It is only when I am Bringing you In that I become aware of your loving, otherwise it is only encircling me and I may not even know that it is there.

Zoe, by wanting to be loved, was confusing ends with means. She knew that she had a Dad-shaped emptiness inside her and she wanted it filled – her end. She thought that the only means: the way of achieving that end, would be for her Dad to love her. In fact it was the other way round: she needed to be loving her

Dad in order to feel him inside her, filling the void.

The Difference Between Loving and Being Loved

A few sessions later Zoe said: 'I see now that the answer to wanting to be loved is to love, but surely, surely there must be a difference between loving and being loved.'

'Of course', I replied, 'Loving is what we do in Going Out and Bringing In our beloved. Being loved is when someone else is Going Out to us and Bringing us In to themselves - which we may not feel. The difference is in the direction of the flow of the loving; who is initiating it, bringing it to completion, and feeling the effect.'

'But, as we have seen, being loved does not necessarily mean we feel loved. We have to be Bringing In the person who is loving us before we can 'take in' their loving. Before that we simply don't 'get it', we don't believe it is happening. It is only by loving that we open ourselves to receiving the warm, being-loved-type-feelings.'

I am confident of this assertion because, though I try to love my Counsellees from the beginning, they often do not feel it: they are too full of their own pain. In fact they not infrequently accuse me of not loving them, because that is how they feel. Sometimes they get very angry about it. Then the beautiful moment comes when they say: 'Thank you for loving me'. It is beautiful because it tells me that they have moved from wanting to be loved to loving.

The Need To Be Loved

'Why then,' asked Zoe: 'do I need to be loved by my Dad? Why aren't I content with just loving him?'

'The answer to the first part of your question is that we need to feel that we are loved because it is our guarantee that if we dare to Go Out we will not be rejected or ignored: that if we have the courage to Bring In we will not be overwhelmed'. 'The reason why you aren't content 'just' to love him may be because you have never really tried it: you haven't yet tried what it feels like to Go Out to your Dad and to Bring him In'.

Zoe looked cast down so I asked: 'Do you feel you ever did try to love your Dad and he rejected you?'

She thought for a bit, then: 'Well he was never around which is a sort of rejection isn't it?'

'Indeed'.

'And I suppose there was his Father's Day card. I had made it myself. He did look at it when I gave it to him but then, when I was helping Mum tidy the living room the next day, I found it in the waste basket. I told myself it was just a mistake ... but it hurt. It hurt a lot.'

We went through a FEE exercise about the Father's Day card and Zoe was able to forgive her Dad. When she had finished and was looking more relaxed I asked the usual question: 'What would you like to do now?'

'Give him a hug'. After a while she opened her eyes and smiled.

'What did that feel like?'

'Warm. Like I was hugging a hot water bottle to me'.

'Mmm', I said and smiled in my turn. Zoe had begun really to GO-BI love her Dad and it felt good: very similar to the warm, being-loved-type-feelings she had identified when I had asked her what being loved feels like. She had changed the message in her Thought Bubble from, 'I want to be loved' to 'I love', and found that loving gave her similar hot water bottle feelings.

The Need To Be Loving

Zoe really had the bit between her teeth now so at the next session she said: 'I've been thinking about this GO-BI loving business. I think I have got the bit about loving giving us the same feelings as being loved. I have been in touch with the hot water bottle off and on all week. But now I'm wondering what part being loved plays if we have to be loving in order to feel loved.'

'Good question. This is the Catch 22 of loving: we think we want to be loved but we can't experience 'being loved' from our outside world until we have experienced the warm being-loved-type- feelings that loving gives us, in our inside world. Our first experience of the warm, being-loved-feelings that you identified when I asked you what it feels like to be loved, is when we feel our beloved as part of ourselves. You experienced that with your Dad, didn't you?'

'Yes. OK, so why do we need to be loved? Because we do; you've said so yourself.'

'Quite right, it is an enormous advantage to have been loved when we were little. Being loved gives us the deep, and largely unconscious, sense of identity and security which enable us to trust. If we have that foundation to our personality we Go Out and Bring In completely naturally: it is our default setting. As we grow we don't notice the transition from simply absorbing the loving which tells us who we are, and that it is safe to be us; to having a self that can choose to Go Out and to Bring In. It all happens as a matter of course when we feel we have been loved'.

'The beauty of the GO-BI loving idea is that we don't need to have been loved in order to be able to love. All is not lost if we feel we haven't been loved. This is because GO-BI loving starts with the decision to Go Out. It does not begin with having been loved. If we have overcome sufficient obstacles to GO-BI loving we will have given ourselves the courage to choose to Go Out – which is what being loved would have done. You have simply had to do it the hard way. By forgiving your Dad and deciding that you want to love him you gave yourself the nerve to Go Out to him and to Bring him In. You didn't need to be given those warm, being-loved-type-feelings; you created them in yourself when you started GO-BI loving. You have given yourself the identity of one who wants to love and security in yourself because you now know that you are a person who can take such a momentous step as forgiving. Through your own effort and initiative you have become a person who can GO-BI love.

'Oh' said Zoe. She was over-awed – as I was.

Mutual Loving?

During the next session Zoe said: 'When I did that with my Dad, I do understand that it was my own feelings of loving, of GO-BI-ing, that I was feeling. And I have felt them again, sometimes when I have been thinking of him, but are you saying that there is no such thing as loving each other: mutual loving?'

'No. I am absolutely not saying that. Of course there can be Mutual GO-BI loving. It happens when two people are loving each other at the same time', and I drew the little Green person looping the little Blue person at the same time as Blue was looping Green - the bottom doodle on the front cover which looks rather like a lover's knot.

'What I am saying is that neither would feel loved unless he or she was Bringing In the other – with their loving. And that each would only experience the other's loving because they know what loving feels like from their own inside sense feeling-loved-type-feelings. I am not saying that Mutual GO-BI loving within a deeply connected relationship is the same as one-lover loving. It is not. The our-relationship allows for expressions of loving, physical and emotional, which are not possible, or perhaps not appropriate, in a one-lover GO-BI loving. However, I do believe that these expressions are symbols of what are essentially two individual loops of one-lover GO-BI loving being created at the same time. Maybe the term 'synchronous GO-BI loving' is a better description of the loving by two people, of each other, at the same time, with all the additional joys that brings.

'Additional joys?' queried Zoe. 'So Mutual, or Synchronous, GO-BI loving is better than one-lover GO-BI loving'.

'I don't think the loving is any better. I have felt an almost ecstatic Going Out from myself and an equally rapturous Bringing In of another who was not loving me. I had all the warm, being-loved-type-feelings and, at those times, I have felt that I am not capable of loving any more deeply. What we don't get with one-lover GO-BI loving is the wonderful sense of interplay which we get when we are Bringing In the loving of another. This does have a deepening effect on our own loving. Firstly because it enhances our sense of identity and security, and feeds our ability to trust and, therefore, give more of ourselves in GO-BI loving. Secondly, when we Go Out for the Second Turn, we are Going Out as a person richer for all that we have Brought In of our lover, including his or her loving. We have a fuller, a more complete self to give.

'The other thing one-lover GO-BI loving does not give us is the trimmings: the expressions of loving that are the looks, the tender little services and gifts, the touches and the kisses, the 'making love'. But, we cannot receive any of this as loving unless we ourselves are GO-BI loving in the first place.

Is It a Once and For All Thing?

'Seems to me that's quite a lot to miss out on' Zoe commented. 'But I do take your point: GO-BI loving is GO-BI loving whether two people are doing it together or one is doing it on their own'.

'But, there's something else I'm not clear on', she added.

'Carry on. What is it?'

'When I first came to see you it was about my relationship with Ralph. I did a lot of forgiving, and facing fear, and letting go of my dream marriage and accepting the one I have. I seem to remember that, at the end of each piece of work, you asked me what I wanted to do next, or words to that effect, and I always said: 'Hug him,' or something like that. What we have been talking about over the past few weeks makes me think that when I said: 'I love you, Ralph' in those days, I didn't really know what I was talking about. Do I need to do it all over again?'

'No you don't. What you did each time was the best you could do for then. It filled in some of the gaps in your GO-BI loving. If you feel you can love more fully now, then you can fill in some more of the gaps. I don't believe we ever stop learning to GO-BI love more deeply'.

'So it's not a once and for all thing?'

'No, absolutely not. We have to keep making the Second Turn, otherwise the flow stagnates and our loving dries up and dies. Once we have said: 'I love you', we mustn't think we never need to say it again. We need to make our loving new every morning: we don't want to love with the same old love we loved with yesterday. It's got to be fresh and new for to-day '.

'That sounds big.'

'It is. Loving is the biggest thing we will ever do and it is the secret to feeling loved'.

BOOKS

O is a symbol of the world, of oneness and unity. In different cultures it also means the "eye," symbolizing knowledge and insight. We aim to publish books that are accessible, constructive and that challenge accepted opinion, both that of academia and the "moral majority."

Our books are available in all good English language bookstores worldwide. If you don't see the book on the shelves ask the bookstore to order it for you, quoting the ISBN number and title. Alternatively you can order online (all major online retail sites carry our titles) or contact the distributor in the relevant country, listed on the copyright page.

See our website **www.o-books.net** for a full list of over 500 titles, growing by 100 a year.

And tune in to myspiritradio.com for our book review radio show, hosted by June-Elleni Laine, where you can listen to the authors discussing their books.

MySpiritRadio